THE

MYSTERIES AND MISERIES

OF

New York:

A STORY OF REAL LIFE,

BY NED BUNTLINE

~~~~~~~~~~

PART III

NEW YORK
EDWARD Z C JUDSON

1848

PREFATORIAL TO PART THIRD

SUCCESS is ever gratifying to men in every object of life good or bad, but it is particularly so to those who aim at a pure and noble object And what object can be nobler or more pure than the aim to elevate the fallen and degraded of the human brotherhood to relieve their miseries and to soften their cares ?

The success of this work pecuniarily considered has given the author much pleasure but a deeper gratification fills his heart when he knows from proofs which cannot be doubted that it has been already influen tial in pointing the benevolent and good of our city to a field where their labors and kindnesses cannot be misapplied

Since the appearance of our first number strange sights and sounds have been heard within the dark shades of the Five Points On each Sabbath the word of God is preached there now and a noble Son of Temperance has dared to lift his voice there amid the atmosphere of gin fumes and to advocate the claims of sobriety This is one of our proofs

Another is that the excitement among the gamblers and other villains increases with each chapter of our work If they did not feel that they deserved our lash they would not wince under it, if they did not know how deep and dark and fiendish are the mysteries of the black arts which we must and will unravel they would not writhe under the exposure

We have the press generally to thank for commendatory and en couraging notices—we will endeavor to better deserve them in future A few have snarled at us but it is singular that all of these have been persons who are themselves connected with publishing novellettes Probably they find the rivalship too strong for profit therefore their *envy* is excited Of them we ask no favors, it would be like begging from a beggar

In consequence of the extreme difficulty of getting good designers and engravers and competing in this branch of *ornament* with books of a similar kind published in Europe where works of art are so much more cheap we have in this number dispensed entirely with illustrations and in lieu of them have given one fourth more reading matter than before We know that this will please the sensible portion of our readers though we do step aside from the fashionable style of be pictured novellettes

PART THIRD

CHAPTER I

Where do you live ?"-continued Big Lize still grasping the hand of the trembling Angelina

In a place they call the Brewery ! replied the young girl

' What ! in the Brewery and alone ?

' No not alone   My mother is with me and we only moved there this morning !

Oh why why did you go there where none live but beggars and thieves ?

Because *he* the wretch from whom you have just saved me, followed and insulted me   We tried to hide from him !

' The villain ! He shall no longer persecute you   If ever he dares so much as to look upon your sweet face again I'll put him where only the devil can find him !

The young girl drew back involuntarily as she saw how the strange woman's dark eyes flashed and noted how hoarse was her voice when she made the threat

Lize saw this and in a softer tone said

" Don t be afeared o me gal   I d rather tear my own heart out than hurt a hair of your head   Where were you going when that cove took after you ?'

' Down into Nassau street to get some work at Mr ———'s clothing store !

So you've arnt your living by sewing ?"

Yes such as it was but we ve had very hard work to live !"

Yes poor gal yes   I know you have by your very looks, but it shall not be so any more   You need not go to the store for work   here, take this !"

As the woman spoke she put a heavy purse into the hands of the girl

The latter seemed to feel afraid to take it, but Lize gave her no time for consideration   She turned her around toward Chamber street, and said

"Put the purse in your bosom, child ! Put it up and hurry along with me !"

' Where to—where do you wish to lead me ?" asked Angelina, timidly

"To find your mother ! She must be moved from that horrible crib   You shall live there no longer   To night you shall stay with me , to morrow I'll find you good rooms   There is a hundred dollars in the purse I gave you   It is yours, for *I* have *earned* it !'

The woman shuddered as she spoke, and while she pressed her hand to her brow she added

Yes and eternal damnation !"

Angelina could not comprehend the meaning of this language. She both *feared* and *loved* her singular companion for rough as was her language and wild her manner, yet had she been the poor girl's protectress

Lize hurried along towards the Points, still holding the frightened girl fast by the hand and soon they were within the filthy, reeking neighborhood   It was now dark, and ' life" began to be active in the vicinity   The fiddles and tambourines were at work and hundreds of dark forms were hurrying to and fro between the different grog shops and dance houses   The two hurried along and turned into the narrow alley known as ' murderer s lane,' and hastened up the dark passage which led to the room where Angelina had left her mother   The stairs creaked under the weight of the large woman, but she hurried on close behind the sewing girl

The latter paused at tne door of the room which she had bade her mother fasten on the inside when she left, and with a trembling hand knocked for admittance

She did not hear the expected response or question from her mother's lips   She knocked harder saying at the same time

"Mother must be asleep !"

Still no answer came from the room and though the door had wide chinks in it, no light gleamed through them

"Can it be that she has gone out and let the fire go down?" murmured the daughter, and again she knocked harder than before

She started back as she did so, for with a creak that sounded almost like a wailing voice, the door yielded to the pressure of her hand and partly opened

The young girl scarcely breathed She groped her way into the room followed by Lize who had not spoken since they left the street

Two steps did that poor girl take across the floor then as her foot touched something which was extended before her, she bent shudderingly down and felt the object with her hand

Oh, holy God! What a piercing shriek arose from her lips then—a cry expressing more agony than words ever can describe

What is the matter gal? Why do you scream so? asked Lize of the wretched girl, who had fallen forward on the floor

No answer came Angelina was senseless The woman knelt down by her side, but when she reached forward her hand to raise the poor girl's head that hand touched a face as cold as marble Lize in an instant felt a dreadful presentiment She arose and rushing to the stairway, shouted

"Murder! a light—bring a light here, for the love of Hea ven!"

But no one heeded the cry—such screams were of too com mon occurrence there to be listened to by the miserable wretches who lived in the other rooms The woman rushed down the stairs to a door which had been half open when they came up and where she had seen a light burning There were three or four half naked negroes playing cards on the floor by this light, but Lize rushed in, and snatching it up returned in an instant to the room above, followed by the negroes with curses, for they thought that she had stolen the candle

When she entered the room they were close upon her heels, but even *they*, wretches as they were paused and fell back when they saw the scene which lay before them

Angelina lay prostrate upon the dead body of her mother, whose face told but too plainly that she had met with a horrible and unnatural death The eyes of the old lady were protruded from their sockets, her tongue was out and the face was blue and discolored   The black marks of fingers upon her neck showed that she had been strangled   her torn dress was proof of the dreadful struggle which she had made for life   In one hand she clenched a part of the stocking foot which had been used to contain her money but the rest had been torn away with the money   Not a vestige of clothing nor any of the provision, had been left even the wood which had been laid near the fire place when Angelina went out, was gone and the fire had been totally extinguished

Lize set down the candle and looked in speechless horror up on the corpse for a moment then raised the head of the senseless daughter on her lap

Water, she cried— go bring me some water !   The girl is not dead—bring water !

One of the negroes turned to obey her while the others crowded up closer and with a sickening curiosity gazed upon the dead woman

In a few moments the negro who had gone for the water, re turned with a pitcher and Lize commenced bathing the poor girl s brow with it and tried to force open her lips to pour a little down her throat

At last a feeble gasp and then a sigh gave token of return ing consciousness and the miserable girl opened her eyes slowly At first she saw only the face of Lize but then her wandering glance fell upon the hideous visages of the negroes and with a start and shudder she turned her head away   In doing so her face was turned down where the light fell full upon the distort ed countenance of her dead mother

For a second she looked steadily upon it then as with super human strength she sprung from the arms of the woman, and screamed

Oh God !   My mother—dead ! dead !   Why do I live ! Alone—all alone now !

"No dear one no !   You are not alone !" cried the tall woman   I will protect and care for you now !" and then, though she had tried hard to suppress her feelings, she burst into a flood of tears

Angelina whose calmness was that produced by utter despair, knelt down without a tear, now and raised her dead mother's head upon her knee

'Murdered—murdered' she murmured, oh why did I leave her alone ! It is all my fault for I brought her here to this dreadful place !'

Lize in a few moments recovered a little from her hysterical burst of grief, and turning to the same negro who had brought her the water begged him to go and call a watchman As the negro started to do this, the others who had come with him all disappeared as if they did not care to be seen by the guardians of law and peace

When they had all left the room Lize turned again toward the dead woman at whom she looked with singular interest

Yes she murmured— the gal told the truth Them features can t be mistaken—there is my poor father's sister—dead, murdered !

Angelina was too deeply absorbed in her own silent, heart bursting grief, to notice what the strange woman said and in a moment more heavy steps were heard on the stairway, and two of the city police entered, one of them bearing a lantern

What s been agoin on here ? asked one of them gruffly "More murder in this hell hole eh? Who is this woman ?'

She is my Aunt she was well an hour since when her daughter went out for work ! replied Lize

'For *work* she went out eh ?' said the man coarsely at the same time moving his lantern so as to throw its light on the pale tearless face of the unhappy child

Yes, for work ! She is not what you take her for !' cried Lize "She is pure and free from guilt she is my own cousin !"'

'Well that s rich That *is* a recommend, *Lize* !'

"Oh God must *my* shame be thrown upon *her* too ! He knows me ! murmured Lize , then as she saw that the men looked with a feeling of interest and pity on the pure looking face of Angelina the woman drew nearer to them, and said in earnest tones

"So help me God, gentlemen she is innocent and good ! Poverty drove her here , they have not been here a night yet

The girl went out for work I met her saved her from insult, found out who she was and came home here to take her mother and her away to a decent place, and found her, oh, God! just as you see her now!

It s a bad business, Lize but you do seem to tell a straight story! replied the officer who had first spoken But old gal, this must be looked into The crowner ll hold his inquest and you and the little gal ll be wanted We ll have to jug you for to night!

"Oh no, do not take me from here—let me watch by the side of my dead aunt I'll not try to go away indeed I won't! One of you can stay and watch with us I have money to bury her decently!"

'I don't see as there d be any wrong in that! said the other officer, I ll stay here and keep her and the gal while you go for the crowner and report the murder!

'Well, Jem, let it go so But we must try to find out some thing about the murder so s to try and catch whoever did it!

'Leave that to the Justice, mate we ve enough on our hands now Look there that ere little gal s agoin to faint!"

The officer sprang forward in time to prevent the poor girl from falling to the floor and for a few moments busied himself in trying to bring her too He succeeded at last, and now, for the first time since she had entered that dreadful room, she burst into tears

The stern men turned their heads away but it was to hide the hot drops of sympathy which coursed down their own rough cheeks

Angelina now for the first seemed to see them for she sprang from the floor and as she gazed at them, shuddered from head to foot and cried

'Who killed my dear mother? Take me too!"

Poor thing! Poor thing!" muttered the men, wiping away their tears Don t fret it can't be helped now but we ll find out who did it and have 'em hanged!'

The girl saw by their tears that they were friends and her fear subsided, but her grief grew yet more wild

Big Lize now tried to console her though her own voice was nearly stifled with sobs

'Don t cry, gál," she said, 'don't cry! You're not alone I'll be a mother to ye You shall never work again I'll keep you like a lady as long as you live!

"Work,' murmured the young girl 'oh God! to call my moth er back to life I would work my fingers to the bare bone! Oh mother, mother why did I leave you!

It wasn't your fault, child don't take on so! I'm nigh mad now for God's sake don't fret!"

The young girl did not reply she seemed almost choked with sobs, and could not speak

Leaving his lantern with his comrade, with advice not to let any one enter or leave the room, the watchman who had proposed to go for the coroner, departed on his errand

CHAPTER II

———

THE parlors of Mr Montague Fitz Lawrence presented a most brilliant appearance a few evenings later than the date of our last interview with him and his family Brilliant not only in the glitter and glare of gas and gilding but in the gaily dressed assembly who, though it was yet early had already arrived to feast their eyes on the distinguished personage in honor of whom the party was given

A *count*, a real *living* count had arrived in Gotham and the *re publican* aristocrats were more eager to see him than ever Mil ler was to witness his long prophesied Advent

On the very morning that Mr Montague F L had read the announcement of the arrival of a distinguished foreigner the youngest son, Gustavus Alexander Manvers Fitz Lawrence had executed his determination of finding out the noble stranger and through his particular friend   Mr Selden, had not only learned his address, but had also visited and been introduced to the Count Delamere at his lodgings

This visit was of course made known   at home   and on the same evening the sons were deputed as a committee of two to solicit the honor of the Count's company at a little soiree—or '*suwaree*' as Mrs F L persisted in calling it—at the earliest possible moment

The Count was also begged to name his evening for an intro duction to *the*   club, for in Gotham there is but one of *the* kind Through these and other sources the worthy Captain Tobin saw very plainly that he was in the way of making one ver grand speculacione and he did not in any way balk the wishes of his new friends in their aims to *lionise* him and to have the *exclu sive* privilege of showing him around "

But to return to the party   It was ten o clock, and a buzz of excitement ran through the rooms, for at this moment the elegant stranger entered, supported on either wing by the whole of the Fitz Lawrence family, the daughter included, for she had been hurried home from her boarding school and dressed in a long skirted dress for the first time perchance with a hope from her anxious Ma, that her budding charms and *verdancy* of manner if we may use the term, would captivate the Count

Some of the company had been sitting, but they all arose when, the distinguished foreigner entered, and the ceremony of a general introduction was at once gone through Then, with the younger son to whom he seemed particularly to attach himself the Count moved around the rooms pausing here and there to receive particular introductions It amused him and not a little flattered his vanity to hear the many whispers which the ladies as he passed made to each other 'what a fine looking man —"how distingue in his manner"— what a love of a moustache' —" what glorious whiskers," as if whiskers and glory were synonymous terms

One of these made her remarks in tones so loud and used such extravagant terms of praise, that the Captain turned to take a second look at her though he had at first passed her without notice His eye rested for a moment upon her, and noted the unusual quantity of jewelry which she wore, then he turned to young Fitz Lawrence and asked

'Who is zat ladee, who is look zis way—ze ladee wiz ze blue eyes ?"

"The lady that's looking this way ?' responded the other— dem it, they're all looking this way Which one do you mean ?

'Zat one wiz so many diamond ! Ze one zat stand up so strait like one candell an' wear ze coiffure of her hair upon ze top of her head like one coronet !"

' Ah I reckon you mean Mrs Smith Klawke She is one of our real up towners rich and *very* aristocratic !"

"Oui Yes sare, she look ver distingue certainment, see how she smile—pah ! I see ze gold in her mout !" The mention of this last discovery of Mr Tobin, was made in so low a tone that not even his companion heard it The latter, **however,** seeing

Mrs. Smith Klawke looking at him very earnestly, turned to the Count and asked

" Shall I not introduce you?   She's a *capital* woman, that is, she *has* capital and gives first rate parties "

'Oui, we will be introduced !' replied the Count, and then he added in a lower tone to himself, " by dam, look at zem glis'n!   I sink I shall make one ver intimat acquaintance wiz zat ladee !"

The two now turned toward the lady, who seemed by her appearance to be between thirty and thirty five years of age and without being really ugly was far from handsome   Her figure would have been passable, had she not forced it into a most un natural and ungraceful stiffness, by attempting dignified attitudes Her complexion showed the ravages ever made by extravagance in cosmetic applications and late hours   But then she was dressed magnificently, and by the aid of gas light really looked tolerably well

When the Count was introduced to the lady her stiff neck and back actually did bend, showing that the lady could bow and with a most gracious smile she received the compliment which the polite Frenchman made on receiving the honor

" How are you pleased with America, Count?' was her first inquiry

'Ah Madam I am ver much please wiz ze ladee of New York zey are very bootiful—ver charmante, but ze shentilmens zey do not seem to appreciat ze ladee !

" Yes, that is too true   Our gentlemen certainly do lack in the refinement which characterizes the French !"

" Ah Madam, you are ver polite !   I sank you for ze compli ment !"

' It is a deserved one, Count but do take my arm and let me show you around !   I know everybody here that *is* anybody !'

" Madam I shall be ver much pleased wiz ze honare !"

The cidevant Captain now took the arm of Mrs Smith Klawke and the two promenaded around the room, while the lady point ed out various persons, and made remarks upon them

That gentleman, said she, pointing to a slim gentleman a little above the middle height, who, with dark hair, eyes and complexion, might be considered good looking, "is my husband !"

'Ah, Madam he must be ver happee ! I envy him his fat, certainement !'

"His *fat* Count ? Why he is very slim !'

"Oh Madam you do not onnerstan me ! It is not ze *fat*, ze *embon point* zat I mean I mean his fortune—his bon fortune !"

"Oh yes Count I understand you now His fate you mean !"

"Oui Madam, zat is it ! His fat in having such an anshell as yourself for his wife !'

An angel ! Oh, Count what a flatterer you are ! Really I don't know but it is wrong for me to listen to you—but I'm told in Paris they————!'

Oui, in Paris you can say ver much compliment to ze ladee !" interrupted Captain Tobin but, Madam pardon me for ze presumption may I ask who is zat beautiful young ladee zare before us !'

"Which one—she with the wreath of pearls around her head ?" asked the lady pointing to a tall, slim young lady, whose nose was of the turn up order, and whose features seemed to have been made in a broken and patched up mould, they were so peculiarly ugly—and then Mrs S K , without awaiting his answer, added

She is Miss Sophonisba Smith one of my nieces !'

No, no Madam ! Zat is not ze one ! I mean zat ladee who is dress all in white an' has ze dark brown curls, wiz no ornament but her own beauty !"

"What that chit of a thing who sits there talking to her monkey of a brother because she has no one else to talk to ?" replied Mrs K , with a contemptuous toss of her head

'I mean zat charmante creature zat is talk wiz ze young man zat wear ze moustache superbe an ze dark whiskare !'

"Oh, she s nobody ! She is an English girl—I don't know anything about her—she don t go in *our* set—I've only met her at watering places in the summer time, where *everybody* goes, you know !'

'Ah ha ! said the Frenchman, and then he proceeded on

with his conductress, who gave him a flying history of nearly every one in the room who was " anybody "

When Mr Augustus Alexander Manvers, &c , was relieved by Mrs Klawke from his duties as a chaperon to the Count, he returned to the head of the room where his father, mother and sister were standing

Ere he had reached her, he saw by the cloud on his mother's brow that something was going wrong and soon found out what was the matter

" Why didn t you keep the Count to yourself, or let our Arabella Geraldine show him round ? You don't care any more for your sister's interests than you do for my feelings—you proggydal!

" Don t call me hard names Mamma! Mrs Klawke *would* walk him off—I couldn't help it! She s always sticking her nose into other people s pies!

" Yes and now she ll take him up for the rest of the evenin' and we won t have no chance to show off our Arabella Geraldine at all! I do wish Mrs Smith Klawke was in Guinea or some other place of worship! She s———'

The remark of Mrs Fitz Lawrence, was cut very short by the sudden appearance of the lady spoken of who had just arrived at that portion of the room

' Your daughter looks charmingly this evening Madam!'' said Mrs Klawke looking with a smile at the buttermilk coun tenance of the younger Fitz L ' The *country air* must agree with her excellently I see she has brought its visible effects with her!'' and there was a very slight tone of sarcasm in Mrs K 's voice

Thank ye she does look purty well!'' replied Mrs F L, stiffly

The Count and his guide passed on, but the next moment when they were out of hearing the latter shrugged up her shoulders and said

' It is astonishing Count, how society is formed here—of what stuff it is made! People do say—and I know it is true, that this same family who are giving this soiree were not many years ago only low grog shop keepers!''

"Pah! Ce'st possible? exclaimed the Count, elevating his eye brows in a very expressive manner

His guide during all this time had forgotten to say how the fortune which made her a lady had been gained—perchance she had forgotten her kitchen days and the honest and frugal relatives who had toiled away their lives to amass that which she was now glittering upon

She passed on but paused suddenly, and while her face flushed up with excitement, and her voice trembled with agitation, she exclaimed

'Oh my! I have lost a diamond bracelet from my arm! It was a three thousand dollar bracelet! Where can it have dropped?

A braslet Madam? You have lose it?

Yes, Count from this arm while we have been walking about in the crowd!' replied the lady holding up the arm which had been locked in his

Ce st possible?' exclaimed the Count, his look and tone both expressing his surprise— what shall be done? Shall we not look for it?'

Oh yes, but it may be picked up and in such crowds you can t tell what people are!'

Zat is ver true madam! I propose we walk around an' look for it, but say nossing an' zen we may be see it on ze floor or in some body s hand!

Well, we will do so But my husband will be so angry if he knows it!

What Madam! angry wiz you—wiz one anshell? He would be one what you call 'em one small dog, one popee if he was git angry wiz you!

' Oh Count you don t know him—he has *such* a temper!" and a tear came into the lady s dull blue eye making it look a little more bright for a moment

Zen I sink I shall do you one favor! He shall not know you ave lose ze braslet!'

How can I help it?'

Why Madam you lend me zat ozzare one which you 'ave for match it, an I will ave one make like it preciselee!'

"But, Sir, my husband keeps my money !"

"No mattare for ze money, Madam ! I am plenty riche, I will pay for it myself, an make it one present to you   It will be one ver grand pleasure, an' ver much honare to me !'

' Oh, Count, you are too good !   How can I express my grati tude   If we do not find the other bracelet, you shall have this and I will accept your noble offer !'

"I do not sink you shall find ze ozzare, zen !" said the Count, in a low, meaning tone

We will leave this scene for a little while now, to return to it, however

CHAPTER III

In the sixth chapter of our second part, we alluded to the strange change which one week of mental suffering might produce in a form of beauty, and we exemplified it by a glance at poor Mary Sheffield

A few days more of life for her—of bare *existence*, we mean —for her heart is breaking, and the reader may again glance at her

We will not now exhibit her within the polluted walls of the splendid dwelling where her ruin was wrought, and where first she became acquainted with her misery

In a small parlor in the neat but humble dwelling of her mother she sat, and changed—oh how changed! even from her appearance when we last saw her   She sat by the side of a small work table on which was placed several books, one of which was open before her   It was the Bible, and as she read it, tears were streaming down her pale, thin cheeks   Her eyes looked as if she had been weeping long   her face was but a record of her heart's sorrow

She was alone in the room, alone with her own thoughts What they were who could tell   or whether the dark and multitudinous things of the past, or fearful forebodings of the future were crowding on her mind?   She had been reading, but had paused with her finger on a particular part of the page, the other hand clasped to her brow, the tears trickling silently down and wetting the sacred leaves

Were not those repentant drops like incense upon an altar? She had been reading the eighth chapter of St John, where our Saviour delivereth the woman taken in adultery, from those who were even more sinful than she

' Oh, God !" moaned the poor girl, " would that I could feel that there was pardon for me above, that I could hear a voice saying 'thou art forgiven, go and sin no more !' "

At this moment the ring of a bell was heard and she arose Hastily she brushed the tears from her cheek, while she murmured

It is the front door bell ! Who can have come ?"

She passed out from the parlor and opened the door for her mother was too poor to keep a servant

A young man entered, whom she spoke to kindly as if he had been an old acquaintance and invited into the parlor

When he entered, he unwittingly took the chair which she had just left, and as carlessly glanced down at the book which she had been reading

With a hasty step she passed to his side and while a burning blush suffused her face, she quickly reached out her hand and shut the book

He raised his eyes in surprise at this action, and said

Why, surely you are not ashamed of this book, Miss Mary ? It is the Bible

Oh, no, not at all ashamed of it, James, but———

She blushed still deeper, yet she could not dared not give her reasons for shutting that book   The truth was, that she, now rendered fearful of everything, had feared that he might see the passage which she had been reading, and have suspicions aroused of her real situation   It was a most unlikely fear yet like a once wounded deer, or a dove which has seen the bosom of its mate pierced, every sound and thought was full of alarm

The young man said no more on the subject, but his thoughts had not left it, as was manifest by his silence   He was a fine looking, apparently thoughtful and steady person   His dress and appearance would denote him to be a thrifty mechanic, or one of the better class of artisans and though he was not very handsome yet his features were pleasing and expressive of amiability

After a few moments silence on the part of both, the young man glanced at Mary, and remarked

You said you had been very well, when I entered, Miss Mary, but yet you do not look well at all to night !'

"I am not quite as well as I have been I have stayed away from the shop a couple of days, and expect to be better, soon !" replied the girl with a sigh

' It is that shop and your late hours, that hurts you so, dear Miss Mary !'

' Oh, no James ! It is but a cold I shall soon be well, yes *very* well !" replied the girl in a strangely deep tone

And then the flush on her cheek faded, and though her face paled her eye grew brighter for there was a tear in it

' No, Mary forgive me for calling you so , but *dear* Mary, you never will get better while you have to live the life you do !

" Ha ! What do you know of my life ?" exclaimed the girl with a sudden start, and her cheeks again were red with blushes

Oh, nothing wrong ! Forgive me Miss Mary I did not mean to offend you ! But I know how exciting and sickening it must be to stand there amongst the cigar smoke, and hear the saucy talk of all those dandy fellows, who have nothing to do but to cheat their tailors drink wine and smoke cigars !

' It is unpleasant James but I do not think I shall follow it long

Oh no you must not Miss Mary ! I came here to night to make you an offer which will keep you from the necessity of such work as long as your life lasts !'

' Me an offer James ? I do not understand you ! said Mary in a tone of surpise

It is no use then for me longer to disguise my feelings ! replied the young man " I love you, Mary—I have loved you long and deeply ! oh how could my passion have escaped your notice I have come here to night to offer my hand to you—to beg you to marry me My own exertions have made me inde pendent I can support both you and your mother Oh, dear— *dear* Mary be mine !'

While the young man spoke in impassioned tones, he grasped her hand with an energy which in itself expressed the earnest ness of his heart

He paused for an answer She had listened to him with an

air of surprise at first, but then her look seemed to settle down into an expression of calm despair

"Oh God!" she murmured, inaudibly though, to his ear ' if I had heard these words three months since I might have been saved!

The young man waited his answer, and again spoke

Oh, do speak, dear Mary, and say that I shall be happy!"

No James, I cannot say the word you wish! I would to God it were in my power to make you happy, but I cannot!" she replied, with feeling

"Mary if you do not love me now, my love for you will soon draw a return from your heart   When you see day after day that I only live for you that your happiness is my only aim you will surely love me   *Do* be my wife!'

James it cannot be! No no, I should only make you un happy!"

'Me unhappy, Mary? No never! Do but give me the trial if unhappiness comes from my union with you I will bear it but do not think I fear such a result   Oh no—do *do* be mine!"

James as I said before it cannot be   there is a reason which I cannot speak, but it is enough to separate us for ever!"

'Then Mary you love another!"

No—as God is my Judge *no!* I love no one now!" replied the girl in a tone of bitterness, uncommon to her

Mary, you act very strange to night!"

Yes James I feel strange   I think I shall die soon! Did you ever see any one die, young man?'

The poor fellow had borne up very well until now, but her strange language and wild look completely unmanned him   He dropped on his knees before her and seizing her small white hands in his bent his face down upon them and wept wept as if his heart was breaking, while his strong frame shook with his frequent sobs

"Don't weep James, it is not yet time to weep for me   Tears are useless get up and be a *man!*" cried Mary, now a little more calm herself

The young man arose, but tears still streamed down his cheeks while he said,

"I couldn t help it, Mary !" *You*, whom I have loved so long, spoke of *dying !* I don't want to live one hour after you have been carried to the grave !"

Don t talk so, James ! I appreciate your love , I wish to heaven I could return it, but I cannot ! Now be calm consider me your *friend !*"

Friend ! oh, Miss Mary, it would never speak the feelings I hold for you !"

' It must James ! You can never be more to me !"

"Oh, do not say *never*, Miss Mary ! Do not say that dreadful word ! Let me live on as I have lived for months, yes for years, in hope !"

A sudden thought came like lightning to her brain

"Oh, could he would he marry me if he knew all and save me from public shame ?' was that thought

Then she shook her head ' No, no , he, like all the world, would spurn me if he knew it and yet—no, I never would dare to tell him

Again she paused Another thought crossed her bewildered brain

You may come and see me James if I am alive, at the end of three months !" said she after a moment s deliberation Then she continued

If you love me, do not come near this house during that time , ask no questions of any one about me, and I will let you resume this subject when we meet again ! Upon no other con ditions will you ever see me !"

Why do you give them ? They are very hard !"

You surely will permit me to test your love ?' said she, in an assumed tone of carelessness

Yes ' he sighed "I will do as you wish , but are you going back to that hateful cigar store ?"

' No, *never !*" she replied firmly

At this moment the bell of a neighboring church clock struck

Was not that *eight ?* she asked, and a flush of anxiety passed over her face

' Yes," replied the young man, looking at a silver watch which he drew from his fob, "it is eight "

"Then James my friend, good night! Remember, now, not one visit to me, or a question about me, for three months from this evening!"

'It shall be as you wish Miss Mary!' said the young man, sadly and respectfully and then he left her

Scarcely had the outer door closed on him, ere she wrapped her shawl around her, put on her bonnet and thick veil and hurried out *alone*

Ten minutes afterwards she was in the same room with Albert Shirley where their last interview had taken place

As she entered he glanced at his gold watch

'You are ten or twelve minutes beyond the time my dear,' said he but better late than never!"

His tone was as gay and careless as if that poor girl had come on a visit of pleasure, not as she did a heart broken creature, imploring means and aid to save her from the shame which his villainy had brought upon her

Her eye was tearful but her voice was firm when she replied to him

'I was detained sir, by one who wished to become that unto me which you promised when you wrought my ruin!'

'What, child? Have you had an offer of marriage?'

Yes sir, from one who loves me as woman ought to be loved purely aye, and truly!'

'Well, you accepted it, of course?'

"*Accepted* it sir?" The girl's eyes flashed with indignation as she echoed his words Accepted it! Do you think I would dishonor a man that *loves* me? No, sir mean degraded vile as you have made me, I am too proud for that!"

'Tut tut, child! You are wild and foolish Had you married you might have made him father——'

'Hush, sir hush! Dare not to speak thus to me! I have made up my mind I will go to that female wretch in Greenwich street but I must have money to support my poor mother for she thinks that I am going into the country for rest and exercise!"

"You shall have it There are ten eagles in that purse

Your expenses will all be paid at Madam Sitstills I have seen her When will you go there?

"To morrow night perhaps never to come away but Albert Shirley if I die my blood will be on your head! *Remember* !

The gentleman turned pale and shuddered as he heard these words They seemed ominous, prophetic, threatening !

But he tried to shake off the feelings which had gathered so *icily* over his soul and with a smile said

' Well well child there is no danger! Shake off your foolish fears I ll order a bottle of champagne now, my dear, and we ll———"

"No sir, never shall you again order wine for me ! I would sooner drink poison at your hands !

Then putting the purse which he had given her, into her bosom the girl drew the veil down over her face, and without another word left the room

CHAPTER IV

SEVERAL days had elapsed after the loss of little Willie Abing don and his parents still mourned bitterly for him They had searched everywhere through the city , had advertised in all the papers but their efforts to gain tidings of him had been vain

Oh ! how many a fearful dream had his poor mother, waking and sleeping in which his fate was pictured

Now, in her wild fancy she saw him wandering off until he reached some one of the many piers which jut out into the rush ing river's tide she saw him looking over into the eddying wa ter then reel forward fall and sink amid the bubbling waves

Again she fancied that he had wandered on unseen and un noticed amid the crowded passengers of the street, until darkness had come on , then she saw him, in her terrified fancy bewilder ed, lost and frightened by the gloom and strangeness, creep into some dark and filthy corner and lay down to freeze and perish

In her dream she thought that there his corse might lay for years unseen She did not know that every hole and corner of this vast city however dark and filthy it may be is occupied

Again her fancy would paint him alive, but it was only to see him ragged and filthy thin and half starved led along by some vile professional beggar woman, passed as her own child, beaten to make him cry starved to make him haggard and used as a bait for misplaced charity

She had heard of these things, which are but too common in the streets of our metropolis, and her tortured imagination pic tured even this for her darling and only boy

In consequence of this she gave orders to her servant girl to detain every beggar that called to ask food or other alms, that she might question them

A few days after the child had been lost, Katrine, the servant, hurried into her sitting room and told her that a beggar woman was at the door—one who had two children with her

With a beating heart the miserable mother hurried to the door to see the beggar, herself. With anxious eyes she glanced at the two ragged, wretched looking little children, but neither of them at all resembled her lost boy

Giving the dark hued woman who led them, a bright half dollar, she asked

'Are those your children, good woman?"

Si—dey is mine! said the woman with a strong Italian accent

But your eyes are black theirs are blue"

'Mine husbant be Inglesa, muttered the woman

'Have you in any of your wanderings, seen a little boy, a blue eyed child, with curly hair?' asked the mother

'Eh? I not know de Inglesa talkee varee much,' replied the woman

'I have lost a little boy,' said the tearful mother endeavoring to speak very plain so as to make the woman understand "I have *lost* him and I will give one hundred, yes, a thousand dollars to find him!

The eyes of the beggar woman sparkled brightly as she heard this, and she seemed to understand such English very well for she repeated

'Loss your babee, eh?'

"Yes, my little boy If you can only find him I'll give you a great deal of money You need never beg any more!"

'I no can find Fortune teller veree wise can tell everything!"

"A fortune teller?" cried Mrs Abingdon, willing to grasp at every chance to hear of her lost one Can this person tell me where my child is?"

'Si! She can tell ev'ry tings!'

"Where does she live?

"Gif me five dollare I will say! replied the woman

In a moment the purse of the mother was opened, and the money paid

'She live in a leet house corner of Grand an ——— street Ask for Julia de ole Ingun woman!'

When she said this the beggar turned away and again the mother returned to her room

"If my husband were to hear of this she soliloquized, ne would call me superstitious and reprove my folly Yet I will see this woman I will try everything to recover my poor boy But I will not tell him, unless I find out something by her!'

This was early in the afternoon In an hour after, Mrs Abingdon closely veiled and alone left her house to go to the place designated by the beggar

She did not see that the very same woman dressed a little differently and without the children had stood on the opposite side of the street when she left her house nor did she observe that this woman with hasty steps preceded her going in the same direction, but much faster probably for the purpose of giving information of her coming

Mrs Abingdon hurried along until she found the house where upon knocking she was admitted by a black dwarf a hideous looking wretch

He led her into a dark back room where a tall woman stood, whose hue, features and form, all seemed to tell her derivation She was evidently an Indian

In each corner of the room the frightened mother saw a large black cat, the eyes of which seemed to glare at her with fiendish and unnatural brightness as she entered

The Indian woman stood before a table—a singular shelf put on a tripod of legs when Mrs A entered and appeared to have been busily engaged in looking over a dirty pack of cards, but upon the entrance of her visitor, she pointed to a chair, and in a deep, hollow voice, said

Sit! I saw thee in my cards and know thy wish!"

Trembling with fear and excitement Mrs A sat down, and then asked

"You say you know my business, what is it?"

"He was a beautiful boy you loved him very much!" said the woman, still fumbling over her cards, without looking up

'Oh God, you *do* know it!' gasped the mother

"Aye! Why should I lie? You would see your lost child!"

'Yes—oh for the love of God! tell me does he live?"

'Julia cannot speak until her palm is crossed with gold, bright gold!

In a moment the purse of the mother was drawn from the pocket and though there were half and quarter eagles in it she picked out an eagle and handed it to the woman who stretched out her long bony, skin dried fingers for it, and clutched it as a hungry maniac snatches at food

Then she turned and taking up four black balls from the table threw one at each of her cats without speaking In an instant the animals came and crouched down at her feet

She then commenced fumbling over the dirty pack of cards, mumbling over some strange, unintelligible words all the while, and finally let one of the cards drop as if unintentionally among the cats In a moment, each of these sprang back to her corner one of them carrying the dropped card in her teeth

The child is alive ! muttered the woman !

Oh, thank God ! But where is it—can I find it ? cried Mrs A , whose reason seemed to be carried away by the singular proceedings of the fortune teller and who now apparently believed in the use and truth of the mummery

The Indian woman again fumbled over the cards with the same gibberish that she had used before but without calling the black cats to her aid After a few moments she spoke

"I cannot say It is beyond my art—the fates will not tell me but there is one my master in this city he can tell aye can show you the boy !

Who is he—where can I find him ?' asked the mother trembling still more with anxiety

He is one who exercises his mystic art for few and is very secret !' replied the woman Before I can tell you—you must swear to be secret and to obey the directions which are given you !

I will swear I will do everything to regain my lost child !'

Then if you would go to see your child in the magic glass of GENLIS the Gipsey king and to hear of its fate when the moon leaves its first quarter four days from this come to this place A carriage will take you to him But he is a king—his charges are princely You must bring five hundred dollars in gold as an offering to him and you must come alone Come as soon as darkness gathers over the earth !'

"I will come!" murmured the mother and then finding that she could learn no more from the Indian, she hurried away

When the lady was gone, Genlis himself stepped out from behind a dark curtain which concealed the entrance to a small back room, and with a smile said

"You did that very well indeed, Julia! Keep that eagle for yourself This game is turning out even better than I hoped. She takes the bait famously!"

The haggard old Indian woman took up the yellow ten dollar piece, and with a smile which looked more like a grin than anything else, consigned it to a leathern purse which she drew from her bosom, and which from appearance and sound as the eagle was dropped into it, seemed to have " more of the same sort' in it.

CHAPTER V

WE left Charles Meadows in a sad state in the eleventh chapter of our last number   Though he had broken the bottle of poison, still his mind was verging on despair

His sister was absent but a short time from him, and when she returned she brought him up some hot tea, which she had made   Her mother also returned with her   She anxiously asked how he was

' I am better now—I *was* a little feverish but I am better   I think I will go out and take a walk—the night air will cool my head!" replied the son sipping a little of the tea which his kind sister had prepared

"Oh, do not go out *dear* brother," said the latter ' 'You are too weak and ill!'

Isabella' replied he I am the best judge of my own strength!'" Then as he saw a tear drop fill her eye, when his tone was so harsh, he lowered his voice and in a more kind manner said

' Forgive me, *dear* sister!   I have become petulant with this fever—I mean no unkindness   I think it will do me good to go out!"

"Well dear brother if you think so I can say no more   If I did not love you I should not feel so anxious!'

I know it, Isabella   You are a good, dear girl!'"

The young man sighed as he gazed upon her   Perhaps he was even then thinking of the disgrace which would fall upon her if his crime became known   but little did he dream of the fearful peril which she was in   He did not know that the libertine Whitmore had almost completed the fatal net which was to ensnare her, that the toils were closing fast around her Poor girl!   Unsuspecting as the timid antelope, upon which the ambushed hunter has fixed his deadly aim, she fearless in her very innocence and ignorance, was carelessly sporting on amid the bright flowers of hope, and the gay pictures of her own happy fancy

Dressing himself in his outer garments, so as to bear the chilly air of the night the brother kissed his mother and sister, and departed   When he left he told them that he would be back early—that however they must not sit up for him as he carried his night key and could enter without disturbing them

———

It was not the fashionable hour for the gambling operations As *gentlemen* always decline *drinking* before dinner, so do gamblers decline *playing* before supper and the supper table is never set before ten even in the most plebeian establishments

In an upper room of Mr Carlton s establishment were two persons, at the same time that Charles Meadows left his door

One of these was Carlton the other his confederate in villainy Sam Selden   The subject of their conversation was the unfor tunate Meadows

Do you think he ll do it ? asked Selden of Carlton in re sponse to information from the other of the proposed robbery and forgery

Do it ? replied Carlton in a tone of surprise at the suppo sition of failure, expressed in the question   *Do* it ! yes, I ll wind him up so close that he would not dare to refuse me any thing !   No not were I to bid him commit a murder !

I don t see how you can get him into a fix so hard as that ! " replied Selden

Why Sam, I thought you knew me better !   To morrow he will be in such a pickle with old S—— that he ll *have* to come to me to get him out of the scrape and then before I give him any aid I ll make him sign a confession of his own guilt, aye, and a bond to do whatever I ask of him !

' But how will you get the suspicions of S—— awakened ? How will you get Charley into a scrape ?

" Read that replied Carlton   It will be in the hands of S—— by noon to morrow   and he placed a letter in the hands of Selden

The latter took it and read aloud

Mr S—— is advi ed to look pretty sharp after his head clerk, one in whom he may repose too much confidence for his own security A young man who frequents houses of ill fame—bets largely at the faro table, and gives large supper parties on *eight hundred* a year needs watch ing This caution is given to Mr S—— by a   FRIEND

After reading it Selden looked at Carlton with surprise

'Well,' said he—'you are smarter than I thought   When the old man raises a fuss you ll lend Charley the dimes to make all his stealings up?

'Yes, on *conditions*

'He will agree to anything to save his name from disgrace"

'To be sure he will and then when he has proved by his books and *cash* in hand that this letter is *slanderous* old S—— will love him more than ever and we shall have a fair sweep at every thing

'That s true   You have a grasping mind, Carlton '

I have *one* mind Sam and that is to be as rich as John Jacob Astor before I am fifty years of age, and then I ll go to Mexico or South America kick up a revolution, and found a kingdom for myself as Aaron Burr intended to do ¹"

If you do, I hope you ll make me your prime minister !"

'A *prime* minister you *would* make Sam ! But wouldn't you rather be the Secretary of the Treasury ?

'I thought that you d hold on to that berth yourself

If Mr Carlton intended to respond to Mr Selden s remark, it was cut short by a tap at the door

Carlton arose and unlocked it   One of his servants handed him a card   He glanced at it then, with a smile, turned to Selden

Speak of the devil and he s always on hand ¹" said he   I wanted to see this fellow before I sent the note to S—— and here he is

Then he bade the servant show Mr Meadows up   At the same time he put the anonymous letter in his pocket, and directed Selden to retire into another room by the back door

You may as well go in and play a game of chess with Hannah to pass off the time for an hour' said he   My wife must be dull for the hour is past when she sends the children to bed "

18

Selden left the room, and the next moment Meadows entered by the front door

"Ah, how d'ye this evening? Pale yet I see but better than when you left!" exclaimed the gambler extending his hand

The young man took it with an involuntary shudder, then as he sunk feebly into a chair which Carlton placed for him, he replied

I'm better, but very weak!"

Yes so I see!"

The gambler rung a small hand bell which lay on the table It was answered by the appearance of the mulatto servant, who figured in the eleventh chapter of the first part of this work

' Eliza, bring some of that old wine which is in the back chamber cupboard! The long necked bottles sealed with green wax!"

"Yes, sir," replied the girl hastening to obey her master's order   In a few moments she brought in the wine and glasses After opening the bottles, she obeyed a sign made by her master and left the two gentlemen alone

Take a little of this wine it is very fine   Osmond never imported better and his stock is acknowledged to be A 1 "

Meadows swallowed the wine quickly and held the glass to be refilled but did not speak until the second had passed his lips

' It *is* good wine   I feel a little better, I was faint when I came in' said he

' So I observed" replied Carlton, 'but as you are better, may I ask why I have the honor of your company? Did you think of trying your luck again?"

"No I am broke flat broke! I haven't a dollar left!"

But you can get more!'

I fear not   I've had the devil in me since I saw you   I've been absent from the store and if the books have been looked into and the cash account reckoned up I am a lost man!'

"No—not so! Have you forgotten our conversation of the other morning? I promised to help you if you got into a scrape?

' Yes, on condition that I should launch deeper into crime!"

"But it will be more safe for you   Your agency in the matter will be unknown!'

"I cannot do it,' replied the young man   'I cannot bring

myself to ruin the man who has ever proved a kind friend to me !"

'Do you think he'd hesitate to prosecute you to the full extent of the law were he to find you out ?" asked the gambler

Do you think he'd pause one moment to consider of your disgrace and the misery which your imprisonment in the penitentiary would bring on your mother and sister ?"

The wily Carlton had touched on the right chord Meadows turned pale when he heard those mentioned who were so dear to him, and he gasped

'Carlton, you have me in your power ! If you save me from disgrace I will do as you wish !"

' Very well, then—I will pledge myself to let you have money to the full amount of your defalcations at any moment when it is needed But you must at once take wax impressions of every lock in your establishment for me You can keep your books up as if you had the cash which you have drawn and lost, in your hands If the old man asks any questions, just put him off, and come to me for the money If he charges you with any thing, put on the *innocent indignant* to the highest !"

' I will do all that I can but were it not for my poor sister and mother, I d blow my brains out first ! replied Meadows

' Thereby making an ass of yourself" said Carlton with a sarcastic smile I never hear of a man committing suicide that I don't think of the old adage bite your own nose off to spite your face! It does not save a man's character to destroy his own life—it only leaves it entirely defenceless liable to every slander which malice and enmity can invent. It leaves a blot upon his name and family which the tide of a thousand years cannot wash away

"But we ll quit the subject It s not very pleasant as the Irishman told the priest, who was warning him of his danger in the world below Take another glass of wine, Charley !"

I will and go home I must go to the store in the morning and I tremble at the thought of it"

' You need not I ll see you safe through your dangers "

Meadows now returned home and the gambler descended to his hell

CHAPTER VI

A FEW moments only before Mr Carlton advised Sam Sel
den to go in and play a game of chess with his wife, Eliza, the
mulatto girl had come into Mrs C 's room with a note

The lady received and read it   While she was perusing it,
various expressions both of pleasure and pain, went and came
on her expressive face   After she had read it she refolded
the note and placed it in her bosom then asked the girl

"Did Mr Cooly give you this himself, Eliza?"

Yes mistress," replied the servant who unlike her sex and
class generally did not seem at all talkative, only using so many
words as were barely necessary for a direct answer

Did he say any thing ?

" He bade me be very careful madam, and said that he thought
we were watched '

' So he hints in his letter   Did he tell you of any circum
stance that made him think so ?" continued the lady

"He said that a gent eman who boards at the same house with
h m and who is about his size came in at eleven last night and
just as he turned to go up the door steps from the pavement, a
man who had stood in the shadow of the house stepped before
him, and, looking him full in the face, asked his name   The
gentleman gave it—the other muttered something about that
 d—d Cooly' and went off '

The lady listened to this relation of her servant, and then re
plied

He may be watched but I don't think so   He is too timid
it is strange to me how I can love him so dearly, when I cannot
but see that he is a coward at heart !"

A low tap was heard at the door

"Go and see who is there Eliza." said the lady, quickly seat ing herself again and placing herself in a graceful attitude

The door was opened and Mr Selden entered

His bland smile disclosed his beautiful teeth and he bowed low as he said

"Good evening madam Your husband had company, and fearing you would be lonesome asked me to come up and play a game of chess with you"

' My husband is *very* kind !" replied the lady

Selden noticed the slight tone of sarcasm which she used, but he wished not to have her think so, and replied

He was certainly kind to do me such an honor but perhaps you do not wish to play ?'

Oh yes I am perfectly willing I was doing nothing, ex cept reading when you came in

'May I ask what work ?" said Selden glancing at the table by which she was seated There was no book upon it The lady saw his look but was not at all disconcerted, for sh instantly replied

I was perusing Lady Montagu's Letters Eliza took the vol ume to my chamber to change it the moment before she hear your knock

Ah yes !" said Mr Selden a little confused That Lady Montagu was a strange woman '

' A very independent one I will allow !" replied the lady She had mind enough to think for herself and sufficient courage to express her thoughts

Therein very much resembling Mrs Carlton " said Selden

I do not know whether you intend me a compliment or not said the lady but in the letter which I last read I remember a verse which you and my husband might very aptly take home to yourselves

Indeed ! may I hear it ?

Certainly—or read it if you like It is in a letter to the Countess of Mar No CXLV in Sharpe s London edition of her Letters, and if I remember correctly, is

> The *man* of love enraged to see
> The nymph despise his flame
> At dice and cards misspends *his* nights
> And slights her nobler game'

I believe it is very *near* the original and I am sure 'tis *appropos!'"

You are very hard upon us lady but if you are the nymph and despise the suit of your lovers, is it not enough to drive them to play?'"

"But I have only *one* lover—my husband You surely do not place yourself on *my* lists, and I a married woman!"

"Lady a peasant may love his Queen, even as he can look up at a bright star in heaven and worship it!'"

Yes and he may lose his head by his presumption!'" said Mrs C in a tone of deep meaning Observing that her answer a little confused the elegant gambler, the lady added

Let us quit this nonsensical talk and commence our game I expect you will be more at home in that than in making love!

"Perhaps so but I would like to take lessons in the last, if *you* would become my teacher!'" replied the gambler

"Sir I am astonished at your remark! Are you not my husband's friend?"

"Yes lady but more friendly to you than him, as my conduct proves!'"

"How sir? explain yourself!'"

Because madam, when I am aware that you receive and read other *letters* than Lady Montagu's, I hide the secret in my own breast instead of arousing an already jealous husband by the report!

The lady blushed up to her eyes She felt that he knew something—how much she dared not think She was not aware that the letter which she had but half concealed in her bosom could be plainly seen so low was the dress made at the neck

His eye had rested on it and he made the remark at haphazard which her confused manner at once told had struck home Following up his advantage he added

"You need not fear me lady but at least in future treat me with a little more kindness Do not act with me as if I were a slave born but to be trodden upon by you!'"

" I shall ever try to treat Mr Selden with courtesy " replied tne lady who now began to recover her self possession

' *Do* not call me *Mister* Selden, with such a haughty air! Hannah Carlton I *love* you! Do not treat me with such cold ness!'

As he said this the gambler attempted to take her hand but she withdrew it and in a firm tone said

Mr Selden I will dispense with your company! Were I to tell my husband of this insolence———"

' He would very soon be informed who the more fortunate lover *is* !'" said the gambler with a bitter smile

' If you will not leave the room, I will!' said the lady indignantly and suiting the action to the word she arose and passing into the chamber, slammed the door to and locked it behind her

By the Hand that made me she shall pay for this!'" muttered the dark browed man fiercely, as he arose and strode out of the room.

CHAPTER VII

Two more days of hopeless misery for our poor sewing girl —the bereaved and unhappy Angelina   The poor girl had seen the disfigured corpse of her mother laid beneath the frozen ground in this time and she had been led before a coroner s jury and also to a magistrate's court to give evidence in regard to the horrible murder

The jury could only render a verdict of   came to a violent death by the hand of a person or persons unknown, &c , the sagacity of the magistrate was put at fault and all the satisfaction which the poor girl could gain was to hear that she was *pitied* Justice was indeed too blind to search out he murderers

Angelina was in a bad place for one who was pure and virtuous for it was neither more or less than the panel crib of her new found cousin   Yet for the time at least, Lize had dropped her usual business and with as much kindness as if she had been a human creature one possessed of a *soul heart* and the other attributes which elevate the human above the animal   even as kindly as if she had been a *Christian* she had devoted herself to consoling the almost heart broken orphan We could not be so entirely *unfashionable* so totally *unworldlike* as to insinuate that this depraved and fallen female could pos sess the same feelings which *others* feel but they were *very* like !

Yet were we to say they were the same impulses which ac'uated her that would be felt by those of the world who had not become depraved we would be laughed at   We judge so from observation from noticing how these hapless creatures are treated by the world—driven from post to pillar by the lash of scorn given no opportunity for reformation, but *forced*, once having fallen, to remain so

Why this is, we cannot divine, yet it is too plainly to be seen

There are hundreds in this city who are heart sick of vice and its miseries who with a kind word and helping hand might be drawn from the fearful gulf into which they have been plunged, frequently by the perfidy of men, often very often by poverty and temptations which poverty and suffering could not withstand

The writer, though young has had the experience of much travel he has visited many of the large cities of the world both at home and abroad but never in all his cruisings has he seen a wider and richer field for the noble hearted and God sent philanthropist than in this city

But novel readers, we believe are not fond of such digressions as these   We will resume the thread of our story

It was as we said, a sad place that panel crib for Angelina but Lize had so far avoided letting her cousin know how she lived, though the poor girl had gathered from a former conversation with her mother, that the cousin had fallen into depraved habits

It was the second day after the murder and night had come on   Lize was sitting beside her pale cousin, talking to her of hope and future happiness when a low whistle was heard which seemed to come from another room at the back of that where they sat and was yet so close that it might have been in the very same room

The young girl started to her feet and trembled from head to foot while she looked around to see where the sound came from

Don t be afeard gal!' said Lize quickly—' It s only a signal from my pal ! But you don t know what that means, gal   Just sit down and don't be scared   Nothing shall ever hurt you where I am !

Again the whistle was heard and more plainly this time Angelina heard a noise as if a board had been drawn along the floor behind her, and turning quickly around, saw that a part of the ceiling of the room had been removed and a small very genteelly dressed young man stood in the opening

The poor girl was too much frightened to scream she stood and trembled in speechless terror

" What d ye mean, Charley, by scarin' his poor gal, so ?   Why couldn't you have come in through the front door, like as if you were on the square'' exclaimed Lize in an angry tone

Cause this ere vay vos the 'andiest," replied Cooper, the pick pocket, for this was he "but who is she?'

"She s my cousin, and a good girl and you needn't patter no flash afore her for she don t understand it !"

'Ow long 'ave you ad her 'ere?'

Ever since you went on to Boston—her mother was killed down on the Pints a day or two ago'

Down to the Pints, eh? And you call her a good gal, Lize ! I didn t think you vos so *green* !

Blast your eyes Charley you're jist as bad as the rest ! You don t think anything *good* can be a kin to me and because this poor gal s mother was killed the first day that poverty drove her down into that hell hole you think the gal must be as bad as I am !

I didn t say *you* was bad, Lize , you needn t go for to get mad with me now ! said the man, considerably put out by her quick and angry reply

' Then just go away and leave us alone till to morrow night !" replied the woman   to morrow I ll get a better boarding place for her !

I wish you would, replied the man ' 'cause this 'ere losin' time isn t vot its cracked up to be ! Ve vants to use the crib , ve ave done so little this veek, old Jack 'll be as cross as a bear vith a sore 'ead !

Well tramp now, and come agin to-morrow night , do, Char ley, that s a chuck !"

"I will in a shake but 'aven't you got summat vet in the locker?'

There may be a drop o' brandy there—go and help your self ! replied the woman

The pick pocket crossed the room to a small cupboard, and, opening it took a black bottle from an upper shelf, which having uncorked, he tipped into a tea-cup which was before him Taking a hearty sip of the brandy, he corked and re placed the bottle then saying

' So long till to morrow night, old gal !" he turned and left

by the same way he entered   The moment after he went out
the panel was slipped back again, and the ceiling looked just as
it had before even as if it was solid and immoveable

During all of this time Angelina had been staring around
her, and at this strange speaking man without daring to utter
a word   But when he had left the room she buried her face
between her hands and burst into a flood of tears

Oh let me go away from this dreadful place !' she sobbed
' I cannot stay here !

You shall go away gal as soon as I can find a good, re
spectable boarding house for you' replied Lize, soothingly
  but you needn t be afeard while you *are* here!''

Who was that strange man, and how did he get *in*, that
way ? asked the girl still sobbing

"I can t tell you all gal   He is an old friend of mine and
them panels are made on purpose to slide back '

But what for ? continued the girl

Don t ask me child—don t ask me, for God's sake !"

Angelina ceased sobbing she wiped away every tear from
her cheek and looked the large woman full in the face   The
cheek of the young girl was white as the leaf of the magnolia
and her thin lips too were pale and bloodless   Her eyes alone
were bright even brighter than they had been ere her care was
so great her sorrows so deep for she was even then suffering
with a burning fever

But she seemed to possess strength as she arose to her feet,
and looking Lize steadily in the face, exclaimed

"I *cannot* stay here any longer   My mother once told me
that you were bad—that you had broken your poor father's
heart and———'

Gal! gal ! for the love of God spare me !'' cried the
woman— I am bad but don t *you* pour fire into my heart   I
have tried to be good to you—God knows I have and I d sooner
end ire the torments of hell eternally than to harm a hair of
your head !"

Tears rolled down her flushed cheeks and sobs choked her
utterance

The tender heart of Angelina was touched—in an instant she

reproached herself for her cruelty to one who had been so kind to her, and clasping Lize who had knelt at her feet, to her bosom she wept with her, and cried

Do not weep *dear* cousin ' Forgive me for hurting your feelings but I was nearly crazy I did not know what I said Oh forgive me—I was cruel and you have been *so* kind dear, *dear* cousin '

' *Dear* oh God bless you gal for that kind word Kind words don t often fall on my ear I m used to curses and abuse, but I couldn't bear to have *you* blame me '

" I will not again cousin I never will speak so again—I never will ask you questions again '

' You shall have no need to ask em gal I ll tell you all now, for you know too much not to know *all* '' replied the woman, becoming more calm

It will pain you cousin, you need not tell me ' replied the young girl in a kind tone

' No don t try to stop me now I must tell you, gal This is a panel house and I have led a bad bad life for many a year I did drive my poor father e en a most mad and he went abroad God only knows whether he is yet living—I fear not '

The woman paused—the big tears rolled down her cheeks, and occasionally a heavy sob seemed to come up from the very bottom of her heart As she became calm once more she con tinued

You don t know what a panel house is ?"

No ' replied Angelina I never heard of one before !'

" Well, gal I ll tell you a little story you musn t blush or get scared, for I tell it to you for a lesson It'll explain what a panel crib is

' There was a woman walking up past the Astor House the other night she was dressed up right smart, and what with paint and false curls and all that looked very enticin like She saw an oldish looking cove standing on the steps of the hotel —a man with grey hair and a rather reddish face, but he was dressed well and looked as if he toted dimes about '"

Toted dimes? ' repeated Angelina, not understanding the expression

He looked as if he had money, continued Lize "Well, there he stood looking up and down the street just as if he didn't know what to do with himself for the evening Well this good looking woman caught his eye as she went past and she looked up at him with a quiet kind of a smile as if she liked the looks of the old cove He seemed to be a little flattered by this and when he saw her look back after him when she had passed he just started on up the street after her She had got away up to Florence's before he overtook her and then he walked a little way close behind her—but when she got beyond the bright lamps he walked on past her till he got nearly up to the next corner looking back once in a while, to see her face Well she seeing this couldn t help smilin and then he fell back close alongside of her and said

"'It's a fine evenin Miss !

" Yes, sir very—but I m not a *Miss* ! said the woman as politely as she knew how

"'Indeed ! said he 'why you are too young to be married !'

No sir I ve been married nearly a month ! replied the woman and she sighed heavily as she said this

'What do you sigh in that way for ?' said the old gentleman, still walking along with her

Because I m not happy ! said she

Not happy ? Isn t your husband kind ?'

I don t like to talk about him ! said the woman and again she sighed very heavily

The old gentleman pretended now to feel a good deal of in terest for her and began to ask her a great many questions

' She finally told him that her husband treated her very bad and spent all his money in grog shops and had gone away to Jersey that day without leaving her a cent or anything to eat that he was a fighting crazy fellow, who d kill her if she complained, and she d walked out because she felt too bad to stay in the house The old covey was very particular in asking her when her husband would get home and she told him that he wouldn't get home before the next night

' Well, then, he began to pity her very much and told her that he had money and would help her and be kind to her People

all that same cove one of the wisest men in the United States
but he was fool enough to tell the woman his name, and the
high situation which he held and she was struck dumb almost
when she knew who it was that had picked her up and was
talking to her She never had thought before that the voice
which had chained the attention of the assembled wisdom of the
nation should be heard pattering soft talk to her but so it was

' Well to make the story short, after a good deal of talk he
persuaded the woman to let him see her home and when he
had got to her door he invited himself in After awhile he
persuaded her that he might as well sleep there as at the Astor
House and she after crying a little kind of consented but went
out of the room while he went to bed

The old covey went and stowed himself away and left his
clothes on a chair close by the ceiling where she had set it,
when she went out He hadn't more than got covered up when
he heard a tremendous knocking at the front door and heard a
man with a very gruff voice cursing and swearing and calling
to be let in

' In an instant the woman rushed into the room and said in a
tone of terror

Oh mercy me ! What shall I do—it is my husband !'

Well the old covey was scared *some* then I reckon ! He jump
ed out on to the floor and while he hurried to put on his clothes,
he asked

How can I get out ? Is there no back door ? I wouldn't
have him catch me and be exposed, for the world ! How *can* I
get out ?

There's no way except the window, and it opens out into a
muddy alley The mud is knee deep ! answered the woman

' It's no matter, open the window ! Anything but exposure !'
cried the old man taking his vest coat and hat in his hand
Then as she raised the window he got his rather portly frame
up into it and in a moment dropped through The woman
listened a moment and heard him crawling along through the
filthy alley and then went and opened the front door and let in
the person who had been knocking so hard

"When he came in, he had a smile on his face, and said

"'Well old gal wots the swag? Wot ave you lifted?

"She took a big greasy looking leathern pocket book from her bosom and a gold watch

" Hopen the dummy, and let s see wot's in it !" said the man

" She opened the pocket book and found seven hundred dollars there in money, and a lot o' papers

She looked over the papers, and after reading them said

' 'These here aren t no use to nobody but the owner we ll send 'em to him, at the Astor, through the post !'

Then they looked at the thimble !'

The thimble ?" asked Angelina who in spite of her feelings had become interested in this story

'The watch gal *thimble* means watch ! They looked at it and found it a thirteen jeweled, double cased regular Tobias so that it turned out the woman had made an eight hundred and fifty dollar haul   She had lifted it out of the old man s pockets through a sliding panel like the one my pal came through and the old covey had been too scared to look in his pockets till after he got out of danger !'

But why didn't he come back with police, when he found he had been robbed? asked the young girl

D ye think he didn t care no more for his character than to have it known that he had been robbed in a panel house by a common street woman that he d picked up? If he had lost seven thousand instead of hundreds he would have kept mum about it   How do you think he would like to have seen a para graph in the Herald or Sun the next day announcing that the Hon ———— ————, had been robbed of seven hundred dollars and a gold watch by a courtesan !

'But this story is not true, cousin !

As true as gospel, gal ! I know where the watch is and it didn t happen very long ago !'

And what became of the wicked woman?

"She s here along side o' you gal   Yes shame that I should say it gal I am the same one—and have been a panel thief this five years !'

The young girl shuddered involuntarily and drew back from the side of the woman   but when she saw that the action was noticed and evidently pained Lize she took her hand again, and in a kind tone, said

But you won t do so any more, cousin will you Do lead a good life now, and God will bless you for it !

'I will try to gal indeed I will !" replied the woman—'I m sick of doing wrong and it's in my heart to be good, but its very hard to get a decent living after you ve once made a slip !'

Why is it—can you not work ? '

Yes gal I would gladly work but no one will employ a gal that has been known to do wrong But I ll try to quit this life, if I can only get away from the gang !

The *gang ?* What has that to do with you—how can it keep you from being good ?

Because gal I m in their power If I was to leave 'em without the consent of all hands they d blow me for some of my work and I d be sent up !

Blow you ? Sent up ? Cousin I cannot understand you '

' Well gal it s because I ve been so used to pattering flash with thieves that I forget how to talk in Christian language To blow would be to *tell* of some of my stealing and to get me *sent up* means to get sent to the states prison ! If I was to leave my gang without they're willing they could give me a great deal of trouble !

I hope then that they will let you go cousin for I would rather work night and day than see you here, leading such a dreadful life !

'God bless you gal you re a living angel you are !" responded the woman raising the girl s hand and kissing it fervently,

I will live right and I ll work too—yes I'll work to help you along Then after a moment s pause, Lize looked at a watch which she drew from her bosom and said

You d better go to bed gal ! It s latish now and we want to go to bed so as to get up early to go and look up a boarding house for you !

Seeing the girl look timidly toward the part of the ceiling which contained the panel, the woman added

"Don t be afeard gal ! There shall no harm come to ye !"

"I am not afraid—I will pray and go to bed! replied the pure orphan

" Pray for me gal, pray for me ! I dare not pray for myself! cried the woman, as she saw the young girl kneel, and there she sat and wept while her cousin prayed to the Father of the or phar

19

CHAPTER VIII

ISABELLA MEADOWS sat alone in her mother's back parlor. A note was in her hand and a few, quiet tears were trickling down her cheeks. They did not seem like the droppings of sorrow, but more like the dews of a joyful heart. Yet a flushed cheek, lips slightly pale, and hands which trembled as they held the letter, spoke of an agitated mind—a heart fluttering with excitement perchance with pleasure.

Her low toned soliloquy must explain her true feelings.

"Dear *dear* Harry!" she murmured as she kissed the letter, "he *loves* me, I know he does else he would not be so anxious to marry me. He says it must be this night. So *soon*—and then so secretly. It makes me tremble. There seems an awful responsibility in making these vows, which once spoken must never be broken until death."

The young maiden paused a moment and seemed to consider, then again she spoke.

'How can I keep it as secret as he desires? It is hard that even my mother cannot share my joy!'

At this instant the outer door bell was heard, and she hurried to open it. He of whom she had just been speaking entered.

Dear Henry!' she cried as she sprang to his open arms and fondly kissed him.

"I see you have received my note!" said he, glancing down at the letter which she held.

Yes dear Harry, and was pondering over its contents when you rang the bell!'

"Well dear one what do you think of it?"

"Oh Henry, I hardly know what to say. This is very soon—and I should at least like to let my mother know of it!'

"It cannot be so dear Isabella. You do not know the importance of entire secresy. my grandfather is even now ill one word from my mother would alter his will, which I *know* is made in my favor now and if our marriage should reach her ear in any way, it would blast my prospects for ever !"

' But, Henry, mother would never betray our secret !"

"Isabella, I would not trust any one—hardly myself I would not even tell your brother, dearly as I love him !"

The maiden sighed but did not reply Her better spirit and the innate sense of propriety natural to her sex, was evidently combating with her inclinations Whitmore saw the necessity of turning the balance, and after pressing his lips again warmly to her white brow, said

"It is useless to think any longer, Isabella If you really *love* me you will consent !"

'*If* I really *love* you Henry !" repeated the maiden with a look of reproach, while her eyes filled in an instant with tears

"Forgive me dearest I know you love me but you *must* be mine !' urged the libertine tenderly

"I will, Henry—I will !' murmured the maiden, and the next moment she sealed the promise with a fond kiss

"When ?' he asked, after passionately returning the warm pressure of her pure lips Shall it be as I wish, this night?"

"Yes—if you desire it !" murmured the blushing girl, and she hid her face on his bosom

" Well, dearest, all will be ready I have bought the ring and engaged the clergyman. He and my sister will be the only persons present !"

Can you trust him to keep the secret ?'

"Yes. He is a friend of mine—a young man who has but lately taken orders, and to morrow starts upon a distant mission to the West. This was one of my reasons for being in such a hurry !"

'Dear Henry I was wrong to wish for delay !"

"Well dearest, it is all right now You must tell your moth er that you have promised to spend a week with my sister, who is a little unwell, and that you will come home to see her every day or so In that way you can get off without suspicion Ah here she comes————"

The mother entered, and Whitmore, rising, saluted her warm-ly as usual

She with kind dignity, replied to his inquiry after her health, and took the chair which the daughter placed for her

I have a favor to ask of you Mrs Meadows!' said Henry, when she was seated 'It is that you will let Isabella go and stay with my sister for a week Poor Maria is sick and very lonesome!

I am sorry to hear it replied Mrs Meadows "Though I do not wish to appear selfish I should be very lonesome too, without my dear child!"

I can come and see you and stay three or four hours every day mother and Charles seems to stay more at home evenings than he used to do!

Well child it shall be as you wish I never wish to stand for one moment in the way of those I love or of any plan which they may form for enjoyment!'

'Then Ill consider it a settled thing I'll be back at sunset with a carriage!" cried Whitmore gaily After a few more careless words, he turned and took his leave

Oh how that young girl yearned to tell her mother all—to tell her that within a few hours she would be a *wife!*

A wife? Oh little did she dream *how* she was to be wedded how worthless and false the ceremony would be which she had so dreaded for its solemnity how cold and hollow hearted would be the vows which she should hear from Henry Whit more's lips that evening

Of this let the reader judge When Whitmore left the house of Mrs Meadows he hurried to the suite of rooms occupied by his friend, Gus Livingston He found that worthy laying back on a sofa with a glass of hot whiskey punch in one hand and one of Paul de Kock's novels in the other seeming to be enjoying both

He lazily arose when his friend entered and with a careless tone said

Ah! is that you Harry? Didn't know but it was Jim Decatur or some other one of *the* b hoys! How goes things? Have a punch eh?

"No I've no time for that I shall want you in that character, to night Gus! I've got everything straight!"

"What ! do you *mean* that which you were talking abou, this morning—the priest ?

Yes, you must play parson—you have a black suit and I ve already got a gown and white cravat for you !'

But dem the thing that isn't all that's wanted ! replied Livingston looking down at the very questionable volume which he held in his hand— I need a prayer book !

I've got that too replied Whitmore taking one from his pocket you needn t fear that I d forget anything !'

Who s going to give the girl away ? asked Livingston, who seemed particularly anxious to have everything done up n proper style

Herself to be sure You and Maria will be the only wit nesses

Where will the ceremony take place ?

In the back parlor at Madame I s !

The old woman makes you pay up pretty high for all this eh ?'

Only a couple of hundred ! Maria comes it the heaviest—she has a *thousand* !

' Whew ! She does take it large How soon is the fun to come off ?

You be there at about *seven* Come in a coach by yourself Here is fifty in small bills it ll put you through for to night !

Yes I reckon yes ! said the young fellow with a careless drawl as he pocketed the roll of bills which Harry gave him

Whitmore then left to attend to other matters connected with his nefarious plan and to make arrangements at the house in Greenwich street for the reception of his bride

His *bride* ! Better far would it have been for her had she been the bride of *death* !

———

When Whitmore left Isabella and Mrs Meadows she com menced telling her mother of some little preparations which she wished to make before her intended visit but ere she had fin ished, her brother entered

" Why, you are home very early to-night? said she, and then as she glanced at him, she added in a tone of alarm, " you surely are unwell again! Your face is deathly pale, and your eyes are bloodshot!"

" It has been a busy day, and I have been worried with my accounts! said he but his tremulous tone and nervous manner spoke plainly of a deeper trouble

His mother looked with a pitying eye upon him, and while she pressed her hands tenderly upon his brow, said

" *Poor* boy! You have to work too hard!"

" It will not be so long mother! said the young man, and both his look and tone was wild when he spoke

But she did not notice this she only added

" I hope not, my dear child   I cannot bear to see you toiling away your very existence and that for so small a salary!"

My salary is *raised* mother!" replied the young man

" Raised my boy! what do you mean?

" Mr S—— gives me twelve hundred dollars a year, after to-day!"

Twelve hundred dollars? Thank God! we can get along so comfortably on that!" cried the mother joyfully

But her son did not join in her apparent pleasure—he seemed sad and gloomy   He had that day suffered a shock which he could not easily recover from   What it was, the reader will learn in another chapter

CHAPTER IX

ONCE more in the little back room of Jack Circle's crib, if **you** please, reader

There is a very choice circle around the old pine table and they are engaged in the peculiarly interesting game—known under the various titles of   old sledge" "all fours," and   high low Jack '

There are but four players present, and these are whiling away the time until the rest of the gang are assembled for it is yet early in the evening

One word of explanation here before we forget it   Some of our readers may wonder that so many of our scenes are laid at *night*   Any one who is at all acquainted with the mysteries of this city knows that New York cannot be *itself* by daylight

The villains who work entirely by night, sleep all the day so do the miserable courtesans   The gamblers and very *fash ionable* young men sleep more than half the day away because they are up nearly all night   The Five Points" are quiet as a grave yard in the day time but noisy as Pandemonium at night   The classes who parade the streets by day are of entirely different grades from those who fill the thoroughfares at night

But to that little card party   It was composed of burglars, three of them being old acquaintances of the readers   viz Black Bill alias Henderson Long Bill, alias Williams, and Jack Murphy   The third person was a new hand to us, but not a new hand in villainy or a stranger to the police of the city   He was about the height of Long Bill but of a paler complexion his one eye was blue his hair light and his face very smooth   His figure was rather slim, and would have been genteel, had it not been for an awkard stoop in his shoul ders   His expression was exceedingly sanctimonious he looked as if he was more fitted for preaching than stealing   And yet he was probably the biggest villain of that crowd   He had but one eye the other having been extinguished we know not how   perhaps by an all wise Providence, to serve like a Cain mark for all to recognise him who have once suffered by his villainy   The others seemed to feel a distrust of him—and their language was anything but respectful as they addressed him in the course of the game

Their stakes were small being ' only a quarter up   yet they seemed to work on the same   principle as if the sum was fifty times the amount   This may be judged from a quarrel that took place between Long Bill and old One eye, as he called the other   The difficulty was raised by counting up   game One eye declaring that he had the most which the other contradicted

Bloody your blasted old ead ' cried Bill   you ave been a cheat ever since you vos born and its nateral to ye '

But I insist upon it replied the other   that I m game ' An ace always counts four   king three   queen two   and a Jack one '

Exceptin *Jack* Murphy and he s a half a-dozen ' said the Irishman with a jolly laugh

But joking aside Jack   said the disputant appealing to him aren t I game ?

Be jabers its meself that don t care about giving yez an anser ould One eye on that pint   If its game to be allers ready to turn states ivedence and peach agin your own pals maybe yez would be *game !*"

There, he s inter ye about a fathom ' said Black Bill gruffly, but why don t yer settle up the game and let s begin hovei agin '

Well I m convenient but that ere quarter is mine ' replied One eye

No more yourn than the last swag you lifted   and when the coppers were arter you left at my door so s to get me sent up you bloody og ' " cried Long Bill ι

'I'm no more a hog than you ' ' retorted One eye " and what s more I've never been a pirate nor served in a slaver nor been transported either !"

There's no knowin vot you *ave* been—we knows vot you *is* ! You re a mean thief—one as dasent call yer soul yer own, and would lie agin your own pals !

I ll pay you for this before you re a month older ! muttered One eye

Ye will will yer? Then I ll do as the lawyers does when they finds one of us in trouble—I means the reg'lar skinners—I'll take my pay afore and ye alf lighted old glim !

As Bill said this he pocketed the quarter which had caused the dispute and hitting One eye a preliminary slap on one side of his head squared off into a pugilistic position for a fight

One eye though his face flushed up with anger did not seem in much of a hurry to attack so dangerous a customer as Long Bill and whatever were his intentions the row was cut short by the appearance of old Jack who waddled into the room, followed by two or three others

Wot the bloody 'ell s the hodds now? he asked Wot s the row? You in another muss Bill? You re allers a kicken up a muss !

Its ould One eye Cap n Jack, as raised the divilment cried Jack Murphy

Yes added Long Bill he tried to cheat me out o a quarter !

Then take it hout in drinks and make it hup replied Circle, in a tone of authority

Vot hever you says, *is,* replied Black Bill but I d just give a mug o yale to mill that one eyed buffer '

Save your fives for other work—we ll 'ave some on 'and for you purty soon," replied Circle and then as those who fol lowed him advanced he added

Put up the ' books' let your game go we've work to patter habout '

Among those who came in with Jack was Genlis and Carlton was by his side as usual closely muffled As soon as they were all in and the door closed Black Bill, who seemed to be quite a business man in his way, asked

" Vot is the lay as you're a patterin on now, Cap'n ?"

" You'll ear ven the time comes Bill replied Jack, then he turned to Carlton and said

" 'Ave you got the himpressions Mr Carlton ?"

The gambler answered by taking a box from beneath his cloak, which Circle opened and found to contain a large num ber of impressions from locks

Any body could know that these was took by a *greeny* ' said old Jack looking at them contemptuously and shaking his head

After looking at them a moment he turned to Henderson and said

Look a here Bill ! Can screws be fitted up from these botchin things ?

Black Bill advanced and after eyeing them with the look of a connoiseur said

They looks as if they vould ! Jack Murphy there knows more n me about em   He s worked in iron more n me !

Not if ye call carryin the bracelets workin' in *iron*, Bill !" replied Jack at the same time taking up the impressions and examining them

' Vell vot s your hopinion ? ' asked old Jack, after the Irishman had looked over the contents of the box

I think I can make a bit of a fit as the ould beggar oman said when she wanted some brandy an wather, and sun sthrokes were fashionable

" Sure you can make screws for the whole lot, eh ?" continued Jack

' I wish I was as sure of a dacent berth in the nixt world ! ' replied Murphy

' Then take 'em and fit 'em as soon as you can, my cove—we shall want to use 'em soon ! When 'll you be all ready with your part, the *papes* and all that ? ' The question was asked of Carlton   He replied

Not sooner than a week, Captain Jack !"

' Then there s plinty o time as the young sinner said, when the ould praste tould him to turn over a new lafe !" said Murphy taking the box into his possession

"'Ows uncle Toby a gittin on?" asked Circle, of Carlton, "Is he gammonin' the swells?

"First rate!" replied Carlton "he made a rich haul I hear at a party which some of the up town aristocrats gave him!

'He did, eh? Who told you?"

My head dealer, Sam Selden, I sent him up to see the *Count!*"

The *Count* eh? a rum count the old covey must make!"

So good a one that you d never know him if you met him rigged up as he now is!'

'Know him!' replied Circle with a look of profound sagacity "there never was a cove as I d spotted once as 'ud pass me agin not even a copper!'

'Ceptin' it was that ar blasted old Matsell!" growled Black Bill   You wouldn't think a man o his size could do it but he s fooled even *me* afore now, and he s death on trappin lush ers and them sort o' crossmen   A cracksman 'asn't a chance to get a decent livin' while he goes a prowlin' about a nabbin on 'em up jist like a cat arter rats!

"It s a blissed truth yer tellin, for onct in yer life!" added Murphy   The rest of the party seemed by their looks to assent to this and now One eye who had not spoken before, but had intently listened to everything asked Circle

' Have you nothin else on hand for us Cap'n?"

' Yes ' replied old Jack, ' but I am a waitin' for that vounker, our Frank   I sent him word to be ere hearly, and it's time now I shouldn t hopen my heyes much if that vos him that's a knockin' now   Jist hopen the door one o ye "

The door was opened and Frank Hennock indeed made his appearance

Well younker, ve vos a waitin on you!   Wot's in the wind? We re a gittin tired o' waitin' to crack the old covey s crib!

You may crack it as quick as you like Captain Jack, after to morrow!   replied Frank, his eyes glistening with excitement His tone too seemed proud and confident

' Why what's hup now, my kiddy?   You acts as hif you'd been a drinkin'?'

"I have!" replied Frank with a theatrical tone and air "aye, I have been drinking from the Pierrean spring of ambition!"

'Vel I don t know what kind o lush that is but it s made a fool o you any how!'

'A fool Captain Jack! Fool me no fools sir! It has made a man of me! Look there sir look there and see a specimen of my folly!

As he said this the young man held out a book to old Jack who took it and after opening it said in a careless tone

It's nothin but yer gov nor s bank book It s no use without his checks!"

"Then put this and that together! Examine the old gent s signature in the book and look at it on this check! replied Hen nock still more proudly

Ello! By the man that played the fiddle afore Moses boy, this *does* look su thin like! a check for ten thousand who sign ed it?

The *fool* sir The very humble individual whom you hon ored with that appellation just now! replied Frank sarcastically

The whole party had crowded close around the young man and old Jack and the latter passed the check and bank book to Carlton to examine

The signature is capital" said he after examining it care fully but will not the cashier make some inquiry when so large an amount is drawn?"

"The *fool* thought of that too!" replied Frank handing Carl ton a note The latter read it with surprise It was apparent ly from Precise imitating his cramped and irregular hand per fectly and confirmed the check by saying that he was going into business again and must draw a large amount of capital

"By Jove you *are* a financier! cried Carlton after carefully looking over this master piece of work

Oh no I'm a *fool*!" replied Frank, glancing proudly at Circle

Now don't hold a grudge agin' me master Frank, for speakin afore I thought!"

"Oh, yes! It's *master* Frank *now*! Before I was younker,

fool and all that ! Oh man, man ! this is thy nature ! replied Frank in the most tragic style

Now do quit yer spoutin Frank and tell us wots wot ! said old Jack earnestly

Well then, to descend to sublunary things I ll take a drink first and then we'll see we ll see You ll acknowledge I m man enough to take a drink now wont you ? '

Aye boy aye ! replied Jack and then going to the door he raised his voice and cried

'Arriet my gal fotch up summat vet for Mr Hennock !

' *Mister* Hennock ! ' cried Frank in a gleeful tone 'I thought I d be promoted one of these days !

' May be yez will some day agin yer consint ! said Jack Murphy

Avaunt, thou croaker ! I despise thy omens ! cried Frank, suddenly turning upon him

Divil the word did I say about oman s or men aither ! re torted Jack but when yez calls for a dhrink o the crater in gintlemen s company it wud be no more an perlite to ax 'em wud they kape ye in countenance jist !

The younker needn t bother 'imself It s my treat all round !' said old Jack who had turned in time to hear Murphy s remark and then when his daughter came up to ask what she should mix for Frank the old man ordered liquor and pipes for the whole party

Quite an active discussion then took place between Carlton Genlis Circle and Frank the three first being considered as leaders in the gang The subject was first upon the present ation of the check which it was determined should not be done by Frank for in the very commencement of their plan to rob Mr Precise they had made a sad mistake in letting him go by his real name In the second place some alterations were ne cessary in the note and Frank was to keep his place with Mr Precise until his house had been robbed instead of absconding when the check was drawn as he originally intended to do

They then made further arrangement in regard to the burglary in the establishment of S—— the direction of which was left to Carlton and Genlis, who had other extensive schemes at work

It was singular how all of these various villainies could be made to work together and how each villain managed in his own way to assist the other but it was like the complicated machinery of a watch or of an army Different parts were necessary and had to work in unison and a gang of villains in different branches of their trade, can always work together better than singly and do more while united than any single branch could do alone

The minor members of the gang occupied themselves with their liquor and pipes while their chiefs were in consultation and thus, for the present, we will leave them

CHAPTER X

On the next morning after his last interview with Carlton Meadows went to his employer's store at his usual hour Though he entered it with a trembling and misgiving heart he was met by Mr S—— with a kind smile and his health was inquired after with a manner of so much interest, that his fears were at once dispelled Yet his conscience was not at ease, the very kindness with which the merchant met him added fuel to the fire of agony which was burning in his heart

Reader if you are one of the *twenty thousand* young clerks who are in this city there is a moral in this young man's course and feelings drawn *entirely* for you Follow him through his career watch him from his first false step to the last and if you will let thought or fancy place you in his position—feeling as he does—knowing his guilt—dreading an exposure and the disgrace which it *must* bring alike on him and those who love him you would never even approach the first fatal misstep for you would more fear the torments of a shamed and burning conscience, than all the chains or bars which the penal law could inflict

You may rob your employers for years in small sums and perchance do it with a cunning and address which will evade detection, but the ALL SEEING EYE is upon you, and man never can inflict the punishment upon you that *must* come eventually, even in life, upon your own hearts After the first step in crime is taken, it seems as if its memory never can be washed away, the devil seems at once to lay a claim upon the committor, and thenceforward drags him *on* and *down*, until he is plunged into the deepest vortex of infamy and misery Do not commence *gambling*, for it begets stealing as surely as words are begotten and caused by thoughts There have been more young men ruined in this and other cities by *gambling*, than by any other means, even intemperance included What more valuable assistant has the gambler than the liquor shop? None! **Why** does each establishment keep the best liquor upon their side boards to be drank *freely gratis* by their visitors? Simply be cause if a man drinks freely and addles his brain, they can dupe and rob him with less trouble Beware' of them all—they are sharks cruising about the world sea and unlike the finny sharks of the ocean they can never be gorged

And yet *gambling* is *illegal!* Why then,' asks the moral reader is it permitted? We echo the question

It is pretended that gambling is carried on secretly—that the guardians of the law cannot find out where it is done? If such a pretence *is* made it is false! The writer can point to many a " hell within sight of the City Hall steps Yes almost within the hearing of the Grand Jury where they hold their usual sit tings there are not less than a dozen large gambling hells where citizens and strangers old men and young nightly assemble to enjoy this enticing and pernicious passion

The writer knows that he offends many a one by this open and plain talk but this book is dedicated to the WARRIORS who are sent to battle with vice in every shape and it is devoted to a good and noble purpose Shall he then shrink from his du ty because he may offend a set of desparadoes—men who are the very combings of society who have no profession save that of genteel robbery? No He has put his foot on the track, and he will hoe his row or die

Let no one then who has these things in charge say that gambling is carried on secretly in this city and that the law cannot touch it There are establishments here as openly kept, and quite as thickly attended, as the free seat churches

Who that wears a decent coat was ever refused admittance o No 3 Park Place or the house directly opposite? Who ever was turned away from the Barclay street hell where *our* Henry Carlton and his gang hold forth if he had a dollar to lose?

The recherche establishment of Mr Pat His'n may be a little more secret because the sons of the *elite* patronise him, but yet his place is well known to those whose *duty* it is to put those things down We intend that these persons shall have no ex cuse for if necessary we will give a list of every gambling establishment in town, from ' Butcher Bill s shop in the Bowery up and then see if it is pretended that gambling is carried on 'secretly —if these worst of law breakers cannot be hauled over the purifying coals !

We do not mean to say that the Police or their ever stirring and energetic Chief are at all in fault in this matter   They are ever busy , no men connected with the city government have harder work in earning their small and but too niggardly salaries But the fault is somewhere —it must rest with somebody !   Before we are done with this work, we will try hard to find out who

But pardon for this long yet *not* unnecessary digression

The morning passed away until near noon and each moment brought more quiet to the mind of Charles Meadows   He had been busy in regulating his books and had as Carlton directed, so made out his cash account that by his books it appeared to be all in hand

It was noon or a little after and the hour when he usually went to a neighboring refectory for a lunch   Just as Charles was about to leave the store he saw a post man enter and hand a letter to his employer   The latter opened it and as he did so, Charles ever suspicious now saw first a flush of surprise, then signs of agitation pass over his fine honest face

Meadows however was about to pass out when Mr S—— called to him

"I should like to see you Charles when you are at leisure Here is a letter filled with very grave charges against you   I hope you will disprove them !"

Sir ?' said Charles blushing up to the eyes, 'I do not un derstand you ! '

And yet he had heard every word that was spoken

' If you were going out—never mind till you come back !" said the old gentleman ,   but be quick Charles, for I have some important business with you   I would like to look over your books !"

"Oh certainly sir   I was only going out to take a lunch , I will be back soon !"

Very well Charles, you need not hurry—I will go and look at your books while you are gone !' replied the old gentleman, eyeing Charles very closely

20

But the latter had now forced a calmness, which, to his too-confident employer, looked like natural composure, and as he went out Mr S—— said, in a low tone—

"It cannot be true ! He has always appeared steady, and I've had him so long, and treated him so well, that he *could* not rob me   I ll not believe it—yet it will do no harm to examine his books !"

Folding up the letter with a tremulous hand, the merchant re paired to the desk used by Charles, to look over his accounts

CHAPTER XI

When we left Capt. Tobin, now the Count Delamere we promised soon to return, and see how he managed with the class whom old Jack Circle terms ' the up-town swells," perhaps because they have been suddenly *swelled* into importance by becoming wealthy even as rice increases in size after being thrown into hot water   Speaking of this last, perchance we may get ourself into " hot water' by alluding thus carelessly to this *august* set   if so it must come, for like old Rough and Ready we don t know how to dodge

It was nearly midnight, and the party had for some time been engaged in dancing to very exquisite music produced from harps violins, flutes, and castanets.

Mrs Smith Klawke had not recovered her lost bracelet yet, as was evident from only one being seen on her arm   nor had she yet deserted the arm of Count Delamere, though, if the truth was known he was anxious to extend his acquaintance.   Yet he had gained *something* and, morover, had received a particular invitation to call on the lady in the morning when she was *alone*, and she had even permitted him to make very direct love

Her husband seemed to view this with a little impatience, and when the announcement was made that supper was ready in a saloon on the second floor, Mr S K. advanced and said—

' My *dear*, shall I not attend you to supper ?"

" No I thank you, my *love* !" replied the lady in a sharp tone, " I am very well attended now !"

The husband turned away muttering something, of which the words "beggarly foreigner !" " dancing with him every set !" ' too much for a saint to put up with !" &c., only could be heard, and these not by the party to whom he made allusion

There was now quite an unaristocratic rush made for the supper saloon, and the consequence was that the stairs leading to it

were in a moment densely crowded   The Count and Mrs S K
were about in the centre of this mass, and no one had a chance
to see Tobin very quickly and expertly take his watch from his
fob break the chain in a place left purposely weak and then
slip the watch into a deep inside pocket, made purposely and
where the bracelet was already hidden

After this was done he managed with his heels to tread di
rectly on the toes of a gentleman behind him who turned out
to be the husband of the lady who was on his arm

Mille pardonnes Messieur ! I beg ver much pardonne !' ex
claimed he, turning and pretending to stumble accidentally
against a stair and as he did so, permitting his body to come in
contact with Mr Klawke

That gentleman received the apology with a very bad grace
even as if he was corned (upon the toes we mean)—but he was
not aware that his pocket wallet which he had carried carelessly
in his vest *stuck* to the Count just at the moment of that press
ure   Nor did he become aware of it until he reached the sup
per table when the Count himself raised an alarm

' I have loss my watsh ! he cried looking around with the
greatest surprise and very earnestly at the F L family, who
had placed him at the head of the table by themselves

Lost your watch ! echoed Mrs Smith Klawke in surprise

Oui, Madame !   I have loss him ! He was one present from
ze gran Napoleon to my fadare   I would not loss him for tou
sand dollare--no not for ten tousands '

' Lost your watch ?   Not been robbed here in my house ?'' ex
claimed Mr Fitz Lawrence in horror

' No, not when we are so pertikler in our set ?'' added Mrs
F L

The two sons sat still and said nothing   They were dumb
with surprise   The Count replied to the exclamation of the pa
rents, by holding up the two extremities of the broken chain

' See zere !' he cried   ' Ze shain is proke ze watsh it is not
zere   Ah Mon Dieu ! zat I should loss one souvenir of ze gran'
Napoleon !

At this moment the elder son of Mr Fitz Lawrence bent forward and whispered a word in his father's ear

Mr F L instantly said

Don t feel bad about your watch Count, if i is not found by to morrow morning you shall have the best that can be had for money in all York!

Ah sank you, Messieur but zat was one ver fine watsh   It was back wiz one likeness of ze gran' Napoleon set all aroun' wiz ze diamonds! It was one watsh superbe!'

The face of Mr F L became a little elongated as he heard this for he knew that it was no common priced watch which would suit the place of one set around with diamonds   But now another alarm was made a little farther down the table

I ve lost my wallet with fifteen hundred dollars in it !' cried Mr Smith Klawke

' Ah zis is ver bad ! Zer must be some dam rascalitie fellow in zis assemblie ! cried the Count   I shall 'ave one gran dis gust for Amerique !'

"The devil must have got among us !' cried Mr Fitz Law rence

Yes or some of his creturs ! added his spouse   I wouldn t a' had this ere for all the suwarees that ever was !

'My husband and myself are even !' whispered Mrs Smith Klawke to the Count

No not preciselee ! replied the Count in the same low tone

' Why not ?

Because Madame I shall ave ze honare of having one bras let made like ze one you 'ave loss !'

"Oh Count you are too kind—especially when you have lost such a valuable watch !

' Ah madame, I would do any sing for you !   You give me your braslet you shall ave ze ozzare made wizin one week cer tainement !

It was easy for the lady to disengage the other bracelet from her arm under the edge of the table, and in a moment more it was in possession of the Count

' What s become of your purty diamint bracelets ?' asked Mrs F L a few moments after noticing their disappearance

" I've put them in my pocket to keep them safe !' replied Mrs

S K , tartly ,   from the way things disappear here, the less jew elry one exposes, the less they are likely to lose !

The red face of Mrs F L turned to a dark scarlet   Her eyes flashed and an anger storm was evidently rising , but a word from Mr F L about keeping quiet and acting *like* folks' seemed to keep it from breaking

The next moment Mr Klawke came to the side of his wife and said

' My dear we will go home !'"

But my *love* !

" No buts, Mrs Klawke ! I *will* go home !'"

" Well sir cannot I come when I get ready ?"

" No *madame* ! I wish you to go now !

The lady looked at the Count with a sad look which seemed to say " You see how I am treated ! but she knew that her hus band meant what he said when he spoke so firmly and she dared not disobey him   Therefore with a tear starting from either eye she arose bade adieu to the Count and left

This however did not take any of the rest away and it was some time before the party broke up   The Count during this time contrived to make himself extremely agreeable to his host s family, and when he went home it was as he came in the carriage of the Fitz Lawrences

Yet he went to his temporary home considerably richer than he had left it and had made a very good commencement to his gran' speculacione' as he quietly remarked to himself

His prospects too were very good and as his polished man ner and address made him always at home in really *good* society it could not fail to pass him in such a set as he had already met with

The Count was not a little amused during the evening at the unmistakeable vulgarity of his host and hostess yet he was too much a man of breeding to appear to notice it   Be sides, he had been rather too much occupied with his specula tions to speculate much upon their conduct

CHAPTER XII

Though when Charles Meadows left his employer's store, after Mr S—— had spoken to him, he *appeared* calm, his heart was almost frozen with terror He could not mistake the look or words which he had received He felt that the dreadful hour had come, the hour when he would either be ruined for ever, or choose the course which would ruin his friend and benefactor and stamp his soul with that darkest of all man s natural faults, *ingratitude*

He thought but a moment as he hurried on not toward the re fectory but to the rooms of Carlton and that moment s thought determined him—weak fatal thought—to trust to Carlton rather than obey his heart s first impulse to confess his wrong, and abide by the mercy of his employer

In a few moments he rushed pallid and almost breathless, into the room where Carlton sat with Selden both of them en joying a glass of wine As Meadows entered a look of fiendish triumph gathered upon the face of Carlton, and he glanced at his companion with a look that told plainer than words could ' my plan has succeeded—he is in my power !'

Meadows did not notice the look for the very next instant before he could speak Carlton arose offered his hand and in a gay tone cried

'Glad to see you Charley ! You re just in time to take a glass of wine sit down and join us !"

No sir no wine for me ! gasped Meadows in a low husky tone, while he grasped the hand of Carlton convulsively 'I've no time for that ! I wish to see you alone a moment !

' Ah alone, eh ? Very well Excuse me for a few moments Sam I ll be down directly !' replied the gambler coolly taking his glass of wine Then as he arose he turned to Charles and said

"We'll go up into the same room where we had our last in
terview if you please'

"Any where' Any where, so that we can be alone'" replied
the young man nervously

The gambler said no more but led the way to the room

When they entered he drew an easy chair up to the table
whereon ink pens and writing paper laid carelessly and mo
tioning the clerk to a seat said

Well Charley what's up now?

Have you got the money I told you I had robbed from S——?"

Well I reckon I have as *much*! What is the sum?

Seventeen thousand eight hundred and fifty dollars'" replied
Meadows trembling at every word

Yes I've got it but I thought you'd taken more'"

'No I have balanced my books this morning and that is the
exact *deficit*

But you gave credit as if you had it all in the safe?"

Yes but I have not one cent there and the old man has just
demanded to look over my accounts' Some villain has written
a note to him about me, I don't know what is in it'"

A note' Who could have written it? exclaimed the
gambler in a tone of innocent surprise which was well sus
tained by his looks

I know not—do not care if you do not let me have the
money I am lost, ruined for ever'"

Don't fret then, my dear fellow—don't fret' I have the
money here at your service—all in different sized notes on va
rious banks so as not to look at all suspicious' I'll count it
out for you'

'Oh God Almighty bless you' cried Charles earnestly and
tears streamed down his cheeks   I shall yet be saved, and my
poor mother and sister will not be disgraced'

Of course not—of course not'" said Carlton, hastily   Then
handing Charles a paper he added

'Here sign that little document while I count out the money
for you'"

While he proceeded to count up a large roll of bank notes,
Charles took up the paper and commenced reading it

'What is this?' he cried, in a tone of astonishment, before he had read a half dozen lines

'Read it all—read on!' responded Carlton 'it is only a security which I want for the fulfilment of your conditions You surely do not expect me to lend you nearly twenty thousand dollars without any security?'

Meadows *did* read it through

My God sir! he cried in utter astonishment do you expect me to sign this—a full acknowledgment of my guilt in robbing my employer of———

Just seventeen thousand eight hundred and fifty dollars I'll fill up the blank I left, for then I didn t know the exact sum! interrupted Carlton drawing the paper toward him and making the entry

But, Mr Carlton you do not expect me to sign this paper? —and besides here is a bond by which I am to pledge myself to obey your directions, in case you pay this money for me!

'Certainly replied the gambler calmly I expect you to sign both documents!

'Then, sir your expectations will be disappointed! I will not sign! replied Meadows with a bitter tone of desperation

Of course you have a right to do just as you please sir with your signature But I also reserve a right to do as I please with my money!"' responded the gambler even yet more calm As he spoke, he quietly replaced the bank notes in his pocket book and putting it in his pocket arose as if to leave the room

Oh villain! Villain! Have you no heart? cried the despairing clerk

I should think I had," replied Carlton when I offer to give you such a sum upon your simple promise to do me a favor!

Is there no other way I will work till I die to pay you, interest and all if you will only lend it to me!'

There is no use in trifling Mr Meadows," replied the fiend " you have but one way of getting the money *Sign!*"' and he pointed to the paper

I will not—I cannot!"' moaned the unhappy clerk

"Then I will wish you a good day, and a prosperous trip to

Sing Sing ! I shall look for the Herald bright and early in the morning Bennett will give us all particulars, I hope '

The gambler smiled as only *he* could smile, and started toward the door For a moment the wretched young man stood as if spell bound then sprung across the room at a single bound and fell on his knees between Carlton and the door

Mercy ! Save me !' he cried

Sign ! sternly replied the gambler pointing toward the paper

Oh, anything but that ! Fiend if you are a devil, remember that you were born of a woman !'

"Very complimentary upon my word, especially from one who asks a favor ! replied the gambler, sarcastically, yet still apparently preserving his temper

The poor clerk was driven to the last pitch of despair He arose again to his feet, and while his face became more and more pale his lips were compressed and bloodless His eyes glared with a light far more intense than natural his form seemed to dilate and swell into a larger size and his nostrils expanded like those of a war horse snuffing the battle storm

I ll thank you to move out of my way, sir I wish to go down and finish my wine ! said the gambler, in a mild tone, fixing his eye upon the maddened clerk

Villain ! will you give me the money ?'

I m very sorry indeed—but can t afford to accommodate you on any other terms than those I've mentioned !" replied Carlton

Then by heaven if entreaty won t melt you force shall ! shouted the desperate young man, and as the words left his lips, he sprung at the gambler with the bound of a tiger

But Carlton had anticipated this from his looks and stepping a little aside so as to avoid the plunge reached out his foot and tripped the other as he rushed forward

Meadows fell heavily on his face and the blood gushed in a torrent from his nose Carlton did not try to keep him down but stood and looked at him calmly his arms folded, and not the slightest sign of agitation in his manner

The clerk heavily arose—but his appearance was changed

The fire in his eye was gone—he was, if possible still more deathly pale than before   He seemed to gasp for breath

' Oh God ! he murmured—'water—I am faint ! Give me water—I will sign !

He would have fallen again had not Carlton caught and supported him in his arms   He steadied him back to a chair beside the table, then rang the bell which lay at hand

Eliza, the servant girl appeared

Some water—a bowl and a napkin !" said her master   " Be in a hurry, the gentleman's nose has taken to bleeding and he is faint !"

The servant did not answer but hurried to obey her orders

The basin of water was brought, also some of the same cooling liquid in a tumbler

With as much apparent kindness as if he had been a brother, Carlton washed the blood from the young man's face and aided to stop the bleeding   After he had drank some of the water Meadows began to recover, and soon was able to breathe freely and speak

" Too much time has been lost, he said with a shudder   'give me the paper I will sign !'

Carlton handed him the pen and paper   The young man took it, and without a tremor signed his name   He was calm—but it was the stillness of desperation   As soon as it was done Carlton looked at the paper then said

" You ve no objection to a witness that this is your signature ?"

' Do as you please only give me the money ! replied the clerk in a subdued tone

' Here Eliza said Carlton to the girl who had awaited his orders ' put your name here !"

The servant obeyed

Now Eliza bring us a bottle of that old wine !" added the gambler

No wine for me —the money and let me go ! said Meadows imploringly

" I ll give you the money of course " responded the other 'but you must take a glass of wine ! You look dreadfully

Old S—— would be sure to suspect something Put a little more water over your face and then wipe it dry '"

While Meadows was doing this Carlton again counted out the money and handed it to the clerk who clutched it even as if it were some antidote for a deadly poison which he had been taking

Eliza came in with the wine and after swallowing a bumper, Meadows started from his seat to return to the store

' Stop one moment if you please ' said Carlton

"What is there more for me to do ? For God s sake, have I not done all that you asked ?

" Yes to be sure my dear boy but just go to the glass there and brush your hair before you go out You look like a fright Calm and compose yourself so as to carry it through bravely Come another glass of wine '

No more—I do not need it ' replied the clerk The next moment he was gone

' Well managed by Jupiter ' muttered Carlton as his victim disappeared This is what I call lending money at five thou sand per cent interest And he chuckled as he took the bond and confession and put it away in the place left vacant by the money which he had given to the clerk

The latter hurried away to meet his employer and it is proba ble that his walk and the consciousness of having the money made him more calm for that he fully succeeded in quieting the fears of his employer and satisfying him of his honesty and the slanderous falsity of the anonymous note is proved by the announcement which he made to his mother on that evening when he returned home, as described in our eighth chapter

CHAPTER XIII

When Fiank Hennock returned to the house of Mr Precise, after his visit to Jack Circle s crib he was a little elevated, not only by the praise which his villainy had elicited but also by the quantity of liquor which he had taken to baptize this praise in

On his arrival he found Jenny, the neat and tidy little house maid whom we have carelessly lost sight of since our sixth chapter sitting up awaiting his arrival Mr Precise had gone to bed His hour for retiring was *ten* invariably and it was now eleven The old deaf cook generally went to bed as soon as the supper things were cleared away, so that Jenny had the front basement room entirely to herself

The room looked very cheerful for the window blinds were closed, the white curtains dropped a blazing fire was in the grate and a very fat sterine candle threw a bright light upon the plump face of the rosy cheeked girl When Frank rang the basement bell Jenny was engaged in reading a book which she laid upon the table on hearing him and hurried to admit him

When he came in he looked very grave but this was caused by his attempts to appear sober Jenny helped him to take off his overcoat and as she noticed that he was so still she asked

What is the matter with you to night Francis? You don t speak—nor you don't kiss me nor do nothin' as you use to did! What *is* come over you, Francis dear?

Mister Francis if you please Jenny *Mister* Francis! Al ways tack a handle upon a *gentleman s* name when you address a gent—*gentleman!* replied Frank speaking very slowly and appearing to have a sponge attached to his tongue by the thick ness of his utterance

The maid looked at him with speechless astonishment a mo ment then, while her eyes seemed to enlarge with her surprise she threw her hands up and exclaimed

" Lord ha' mercy on us ! Why what has come over you all to onct ?

"Nothing Jenny—nothing has come over *me*—nothing can me overcome ! cried Frank steadying himself by the table to keep from falling

' Why you've been a drinkin' ! Oh, if master should find it out ! '

Ay there s the rub ! But Jenny my dear he won t unless you speak to him in stenography my dear !

' In stenography ! what's that ? '

" What ! you don t know what st—stenography is ? Well, it's like politics—the principles of ninety six ' You know what they are don t you ?

The maid shook her head negatively

' Then I won't talk to such an ignoramus ! ' replied Frank, loftily

This was too much for Jenny   She burst into a flood of tears and amid broken intervals of sobbing said—

' It's too bad it is, to be called hard names by one as I loved so true and sweet   If it weren't for you I d be the most vartuesest girl in all York, so I would ! You ve got my love, and—and——"

Here her sobs rendered her words inaudible

Becoming a little more calm she continued

' I s pose you ll desart me now ! Oh, my ! oh, my ! I wish I was dead afore ever I saw you ! I ll go and jump off the dock, I will ! I ll take *pison,* so I will ! "

Frank had stood and listened all the time very quietly, but when she made the last remark, a sudden thought seemed to strike his brain   Assuming a tragic air, he cried

' Ah ! is it thou my Juliet ? Methinks I stand within the tomb of the Capulets ! '

' Oh, you needn't come any of that over me now ! ' sobbed the girl, ' after abusin me like as you have ! There I was awaitin' for you to come, a studyin' out Juliet, and spellin' the hard words apurpose to act with you, and here I am abused as if I was a cat ! "

With this her tears and sobs broke out afresh But Frank now assumed the tender

' *Don't* weep Jenny Thy tears are pearls! Give them not unto the thirsty carpet!"

"I will cry, so I will! You called me hard names, when I don t desarve none as you haven t been the cause of!" replied the girl

'Well, Jenny I won t do so any more! I was a little elevat ed , I had been thinking of——let me see what was it? I say Jenny don t you think Paul Clifford was a great man—a hero?"

I never knowed him!" replied the girl whose tears now became more scarce

' But did you never read of him?'

'No—I never read nothin' but my spellin' book and primmer, what tells that Zaccheus he did climb the tree his Lord to see, and John Rogers and his nine children at the breast burnt into a steak till you showed me that 'ere!

As she spoke she pointed to the volume of Shakspeare, which lay upon the table Frank seated himself now, and reaching for the book, said

So you were reading your part, Juliet!'

'Yes, Frank, and I had it so good, but now you've scared it all out of me!"

Don't call me Frank Juliet! my name is Romeo, on the Grampus hills my father—no, I forget, I m an Italian I say, Juliet let's begin the garden scene He jests at wounds that never felt a scar!

'No," replied Jenny, 'I don't like that half so well as the chamber scene!'

"Oh, Juliet—Juliet! The woman will out in thee—but I say, what's o'clock?"

It isn t day it s the nightly gale that pierced your hollow ear out of the pounded granite tree Believe—"

"Oh, blast the thing, Juliet my love you're out!"

'No, my sweet lord—I read it in the book indeed I did, good Romeo!"

" Just let Romeo drop and go and see what o'clock it is! I'm sleepy!"

"Yon light is not daylight I know it—'

No blast it no ! It s the candle one of the old man's own
patterns !

'Oh my Francis ! If he should hear you call him the *old
man* !

Well what if he should ? He isn t anything else !' replied
Frank rising and steadying himself by the table   Then, after
looking at Jenny a moment he said

I think its time to go to bed—to retire and court those slum
bers which bless innocence and beauty ''

You used to be fonder of courtin me !' murmured Jenny,
but now you don t care for me at all ! That s the way—a
poor girl may do all she can to please a man and then in a
little while he ll go away and leave her !''

She paused a moment to wipe away a tear with one corner
of her apron then clasping her arms around his neck affection
ately cried

Oh, my Romeo—why *be* you Romeo !

Thunder and Mars ! Ye Gods ! Must I bear all this?'
cried Frank with a sudden start   Blast it drop your Ro
meo s !

The start and his tone so frightened poor Jenny that she
sprung back and literally obeyed him for when he lost the support of her arms he *dropped* full length on the floor

Oh my gracious He *is* drunk ! said Jenny, as she endea
vored to raise his limber form

Yes—yes muttered Frank stupidly— here on the ground
with my own tears made drunk   A decided and unmistakeable
Rummyo ! Ha ! ha ! That was a good joke—wasn't it Cap n
Jack ?

Oh my what can he mean by Cap n Jack ? I do wish I
could get him up to bed   Frank Frank—get up !

Don t disturb the king ! He s d de cidedly averse to receiving
the dose ! muttered Frank evidently fast sinking into a stupid
lethargy

The girl paused a moment to think what was best to do, then
stooping down she raised him up and balancing his body across
her right shoulder, with his feet hanging down nearly to the

floor at her heels and his head quite as low in front, she started off for his bed room

He was slim and lean, though tall, and therefore was not a very heavy load for her stout frame Though he was too far gone to know how he was moving, he seemed to be aware that he was in *transitu*, for he murmured

' Th this s side up with care, and k keep dry !"

"I wish you'd keep dry rather than to get drunk Oh, if master *should* find it out, he d lose his place and I'd lose my beau !" murmured Jenny as she left the room.

21

CHAPTER XIV

It was evening twilight, we mean, on the fourth day after Mrs Abingdon had visited the Indian fortune teller Mr A had been absent all day on a trip to a neighboring town for still he kept up the search, day after day for his lost boy He had not yet returned and as darkness began to come on Mrs A put on her bonnet veil and thick cloak then calling her servant said

' Katrine, I am going out to spend the evening with a friend if your master comes home before I do tell him not to be alarmed, I will come back in a carriage '

The girl replied, and the next moment Mrs A was on her way to the Indian fortune teller s as fast as her feeble limbs would carry her On arriving at the house she saw that a carriage was indeed in waiting and also noticed that the horses harnessed before it were not matched in color one being dark the other white It looked more like a common hack, too than a private coach

But she did not pause to look at it, only noticing the peculiarity in a glance, while she knocked at the door which once before had been opened unto her

The same dwarf appeared to admit her, and she next found herself before the Indian woman

You are here and ready '* said the Indian

I am but let me go quickly I wish to find out about my child and get home before my husband returns ''

' You need not fear, returned the fortune teller ' He will not be home until nearly two o clock '

"What ! so late? How can you tell—where is he ? '

"He is now in a small town in New Jersey 'He will return, by the Philadelphia late train of cars '"

"Oh, heaven ! How strange is this ! how can you tell ?"

"Woman ask not how, only mark that which I say *is!*" re-
ied the fortune teller

But my child , when can I go to this man, whom you call your
aster ?   asked the lady

Have you brought his offering ?"

If you mean the money I have it here   There are five hun
'ed dollars in that purse ' replied Mrs A   handing the woman
purse which was round with its fullness

The woman took it and went behind the curtain of the back
om   While she was absent Mrs A   heard whispering, and
.e clink of the gold as it was counted out but before she could
:volve the reason of these whisperings in her mind the woman
:turned

"The offering is good—the amount right   she said,   you
.all now go to GENLIS the king of all the Gipseys in America
.is mirror will show thee thy boy wherever he may be !

"Oh haste then to take me there !"

"I will lady but you must first be blindfolded "

"Anything—anything to see my lost Willie !" And then
.e lady permitted a large black shawl to be bound tightly
round her head covering her eyes with several folds   only
.aving her room to breathe freely

The moment after this was done the voice of a man was
eard close by her side , not a gruff or discordant tone, but soft
nd calm even as gentle as that used by her own husband in
.s fondest moods

' Come lady   said the man "take my arm and fear not ,
ou are under my care and protection ' '

There was something in his tone even more soothing to one
) nervous as Mrs A   than the harsh tones of the Indian,
.ough she trembled she clung to the arm through which he
.laced hers

' To the carriage now—it will not take very long !" added the
.an and she walked on soon finding by the cold air that she
.as in the street next finding herself gently lifted into the car
.age

Her conductor entered, seated himself by her side, and, with out having received any audible orders, the driver started off at a very rapid speed

The person who sat with Mrs A seemed from his address to be a man of genteel manners and general information and as the carriage hurried on, endeavored to open a conversation But she was too frightened to more than answer his remarks by monosyllabic expressions and he soon became silent

The carriage all this time seemed to be driven at a rapid rate and Mrs A supposed that she was driving directly out of the city After full an hour had passed she ventured to ask of her companion

"Are we not nearly there ?"

Yes within about a mile ! replied the man and the carriage kept on still jolting over the paving stones, when from the distance gone it ought to have been out upon some unpaved road

For full a quarter of an hour more the carriage kept on, but at the expiration of this time they stopped

Her conductor quickly alighted, and before he handed her out of the carriage went to speak to the driver

She took advantage of this moment of non surveillance to draw her scissors from her pocket and cut a single cord from the tassel of the coach which hung on the side next to her and to replace the scissors and cord in her pocket before the man returned

This though it occupied not ten seconds was scarcely done before her conductor was again at the coach door

You will alight here madam !" he said, and then he reached out his hand to assist her in doing so

"She took his arm after getting upon the pavement, and soon judged from the absence of fresh air that she was entering an alley Next her guide paused, and by the sound of a bell rung by him she judged that she was at a door She was right, for she heard the door swing on its hinges, then as they advanced she felt a carpet under her feet In another instant they commenced ascending stairs, then after walking along a carpeted passage they decended stairs, and in a moment were in the open air again but not apparently passing through the door by which they had entered

' What does all this mystery mean ?" asked the lady, beginning to be frightened

"Genlis the King wishes it !" replied her guide, " do not fear, there is no danger !

They went on but Mrs A supposed by the feeling of the cold air as well as by the brick pavement beneath her feet that she was again in the street Yet this was not the case as subsequent pages will prove But they went on and on until Mrs A became impatient thinking that she had already walked several blocks

' Have we not nearly arrived at the place ?' she murmured, I am so tired !

' Ten steps more fair lady and we are there replied her guide

The steps seemed short ones to her for she was conscious of entering a door the next moment, and after passing but a little way, found herself seated carefully on a soft and yielding sofa

Then a female voice addressed her in a tone of uncommon sweetness

' Are you fatigued or frightened lady ?"

' I am tired but are we there ?

' You are in the dwelling of Genlis !" replied the voice

' Then let me see my child May I take this bandage from my eyes ?

Count one thousand, silently but truly ' replied the stranger, " then remove it !

The lady was about to commence, when again the other female spoke

You must remember " said she " not to speak, whatever you may see else the charm will dissolve in an instant ! You would see a child, a blue eyed, golden haired boy, whom you have lost ?'

I would ! replied Mrs A rapidly recovering her presence of mind, with the assurance that one of her own sex was near

" Then,' replied the other " be calm—see, but do not open

your lips ! Count on, and when the thousand is told, take off
your veil !

Audibly but with a trembling voice, did the poor mother com
mence counting ten hundred units   How long seemed to her
the time   how slowly her powers of utterance seemed to work
But she finished

With a tremulous hand she untied the bandage which covered
her eyes   When this was done, a blaze of light, coming she
could not see from where seemed to blind her but either the
light grew more dim, or she soon got more used to it for she
could now look around the room   It was of an oblong shape,
and hung altogether with black   A chill ran through every vein
of Mrs A   when she saw this, for it at once seemed ominous of
the death of her child but ere these thoughts had time to settle
into her almost fear frozen heart she saw at the upper end of
the room a beautiful being which looked more like an angel
than a being of earth

It appeared to be a woman for a woman's peerless form her
swelling bosom tapering waist full lips and limbs at once
voluptuous yet delicate were there but too slightly hidden by
a light gauze short dress such as is worn by the stage dancers,
even much more transparent   Woman as she was Mrs A
blushed as she looked yet gazed at this beautiful vision   It did
not move—it seemed to be a statue or a wax figure   If so it
was indeed perfect   As it was turned quarter face toward her,
Mrs A saw that it had large black, mournful looking eyes,
that seemed turned toward heaven even as if in prayer its
lashes were long and silky its hair curling and jetty black   In
complexion it was very clear yet not so fair, nor so pale as
even Mrs A was   Yet in symmetry of figure it was perfect

She looked at it' in silent surprise, for she remembered her
warning not to speak   She then noted that it stood close to the
upper end of the room some forty or fifty feet from her, and
close beside a curtain of black velvet which hung over that end
of the room

While she still gazed in silent astonishment upon this beauti
ful creature a deep heavy, but not unmusical voice was heard
close beside her saying

"So this daughter of mortals would test the skill of Genlis ?"

She turned quickly and saw by her side a very tall and sin gular looking man whose dress was as odd and quite in unison with his personal appearance He was we have just said, rather tall his eyes were black as night—his complexion as dark as a Moor s (not quite as dark as the *negro* Othello s of our present theatre s), and his look stern and commanding

The poor lady trembled as she gazed, she could not speak She glanced again at the person—saw that his dress was of Turkish or Persian style, she did not know which and as his face seemed to unbend its sternness beneath her fearful and im ploring gaze she gathered strength to say

If you are this Genlis the Gipsey king do show me my child !

'Daughter beware, and dare not to speak or move ! One word or motion will be enough to break the charm !"

As he said this the strange being moved a wand which he held in his hand and as he did so the beautiful vision at the upper end of the room knelt upon the floor Then the curtain slowly rose disclosing to the anxious mother a plain mirror—a very large one occupying the upper end of the room When the cur tain had been rolled up to the ceiling which seemed to be done by invisible hands Mrs A noticed that a kind of fog or smoke seemed fast gathering over the face of the mirror Still she looked on until the mirror bore the appearance of a sky through which the white scud of the wild storm is flying Then when her heart had become almost still from fear and anxiety the clouds seemed to stop and right in their midst arose a form—the form of a young child Oh how she gazed at it while yet the clouds seemed to hide some of its proportions but in a few mo-ments it was plainly visible

There he stood her own Willie dressed in the very clothes ! which he had worn when she had last seenhim—garments proudly made by her own hands there with his glad blue eyes and bright brown hair He seemed to look a little more pale ; but even this might have been fancy with her

Tell a mother not to speak or move under such circumstances !

Better bid the ocean go to sleep, or the northwest blast to hold its peace!

She gazed one long, long minute She was satisfied that it was he

She gave one wild shriek

'My child! my child! it *is* my boy!" then rushed toward the spot As she did so she heard a noise like the hissing of a serpent—then a rumbling, like distant thunder Her strength failed! she trembled—fell to the floor!

It might have been but a minute, it might have been an hour that she was insensible she knew not how long, for when she recovered Genlis the Gipsey King, was bending over her, applying restoratives, such as are commonly used

The curtain was still up—the angelic form still knelt close beside it and the mirror was yet in view But the latter was plain nothing but the bright glass could be seen

As she came to her senses the lady murmured

Where has he gone? Oh, it was him! it was him!'

Lady I warned you not to speak or move!" replied Genlis "you broke the charm!'

"Then was it not real?

I may not say, but had you remained still, you would have learned more!

Oh try it once more I will not even breathe!" murmured the mother

"I cannot now If you would again look in the Magic Mirror it must be at another time!"

When oh when? I will indeed look at it again!'

"Then be where you entered the carriage to night, four evenings from now!

I will—I will!' replied the lady "Oh why did I speak!"

It cannot now be helped, lady The Fates willed it be patient and hopeful you yet may see and recover your child, but it will be after many trials and much expense!"

'I care not oh I care not so that I once more may clasp him to my arms! replied the mother

"You shall replied the Gipsey, "but it is all over for this time you must again be veiled and return as you came!"

" But, why all this mystery ?"

" Because this is a land of stern laws and great unbelief!
We must be secret ! You have sworn to keep this visit and its
sights a secret even from your husband Pledge me the same,
even as you did Julia !"

' Why—why must I keep it from *him* ? '

' It is enough that you must ! Promise, or you shall never
see your infant more ! '

" I promise !" murmured the woman

The Gipsey now proceeded to veil her as before then she was
led out into the air and after walking a short distance, replaced
in the carriage It was driven off very fast and now there
seemed to be no one inside of the coach with her She how
ever did not move or speak and for an hour the coach rattled
along while she sat trembling in it

At last it stopped the steps were let down, and a man hav
ng the Irish brogue on his tongue said

" You can get out here ma am !

She did so and while she waited to have the bandage pulled
from her eyes, she heard the steps put up the carriage door
shut to and then heard it rattle along the pavement as it was
driven rapidly off

She then dared to take off the bandage herself To her sur
prise she found herself before her own door Had it not been
for the black shawl in her hands and the distant rattling of the
receding carriage she would have believed herself in a dream,
but she could not All had been but too real and moreover,
reader, strange as is this mystery it is no *romance* as the se
quel will prove, no formation of our fancy but a true account
of a real occurrence in this city It may now appear strange
and supernatural, we will see by and bye how it will look

When Mrs A rang the bell and was admitted by Katrine
she asked for her husband He had not yet returned home
She began indeed now to believe all she had seen and heard,
though she never had been superstitious before

CHAPTER XV

WHEN Carlton had dismissed Meadows, after securing the bond, he returned to his confederate Selden

Succeeded ? asked the dark browed villain

He needed not to inquire—the look of triumph gleaming from Carlton s eyes was enough to tell him that he had not failed

Of course " replied the gambler, " when did I ever fail in any thing I tried to turn my hand to ? '

How did he act—did he take the conditions easily ?"

' About as easily as a spoiled child takes ipecac   First a fit of the sullen—then a trial of the pathetic—to close up, a grand effort at the tragic —— "

" Which you —— '

' Tripped in an instant   When he found it was my conditions or no money he concluded to sell himself   He is now my *slave*— he dare not call his soul his own ! '

' By Jove but you should have been a king—you would have lorded it nobly on a throne ! ' cried Selden, apparently in real admiration of the deep villainy of his master

I would if I had been born as the Czar of Russia lord over the lives of millions of subjects   Then I would have *kinged* it, indeed for there should be no *will* but *mine* no eye that dare to gaze upon me without I willed it   Then, we would see whether I would be spurned hated scorned, as I am now simply because I am a *gambler* ! I can t go into the best society, why ? because I am a sporting man   Men, merchants and aristocrats will come here to my rooms and play with me—they will drink wine and eat at my table they meet and shake hands with me, *here*, but when I meet them in the street, the *gentlemen* cannot recognise me   They find it impossible to remember where they have met me   They never invite me to their houses Though my wife is perhaps as well educated, and as agreeable as any of theirs she never can be invited out to see them   Curse such consistency say I, if they can associate with me at one time, I can t see why they should not others! I don't care so much for myself as I do for the sake of my wife!

"She manages to do very well" replied Selden with apparent carelessness   I reckon she s not much at a loss for company!

'Company Sam? Why she hardly ever goes out and ——'

Excepting in the evening pretty often! replied Selden still in h s careless tone interrupting Carlton

In the evening! Why Sam what are you talking about? This very morning my wife told me that she was sick and tired of living so lonely—that she had not been out of the house once for ten days!

Indeed! exclaimed Selden in a tone very expressive of doubt

Yes   do you know to the contrary?

Why if she *says* so it s against my rule to contradict a *lady*, but—— never mind we ll drop the subject! replied Selden still more careless in his apparent tone   Yet he was using the very means to fan the flame to awake the sleeping jealousy of that fiery husband and well he knew it

The husband looked him sternly in the eye for a moment after he had last spoken then while his face grew a shade more pale than usual if possible and his blue lip quivered with excite ment he said in a husky voice

'Sam, don t put the devil in me! I know that woman but I've not been jealous of her lately—I hope I ve no cause to be!'

I *hope* not! replied the Iago still in his quiet insinuating tone

You *hope* not! Sam you mean something yes by Heaven you *know* something! Are you my friend?

'If you don t know that and cannot judge me by an intimacy of years my words will never satisfy you of it!

Right Sam right   Yes I know and have often proved your friendship   I m calm now—go on and tell me all   You know something about my wife?

Carlton said that he was calm   He was so, calm as the full charged storm cloud full almost to bursting with lightning and thunder and the sweeping wind which bows the forest, calm as that cloud when it settles down towards the earth and hides the face of heaven from the terrified worms of mortality

Selden saw this and his following hesitation only served to add to the power of the storm

Speak—don t trifle with me ! If you know anything about her, tell me of it ! cried Carlton, evidently becoming each mo ment more agitated

Don t get excited my friend ' cried Selden— don t get ex cited I ve not said that I knew anything !

'No, you have not *said* it—but l know you do   Now do tell me that s a good fellow Sam I ll be calm—calm as if I was at the board with a big game on hand   See I m calm and quiet now   I was a little excited for a moment but I m quiet as a lamb now !

If quivering lips, eyes reddened and flashing with but half suppressed excitement the muscles of the face twitching as with spasmodtic convulsions the hands clutched until the blood seemed about to burst from beneath the finger nails, the whole frame of the man trembling—denoted calmness then was that villainous gambler calm

However Selden had his game to play and well did he know, —thief murderer wretch libertine accomplished as he was in all the phases of villainy—how to play it   His eye lustful, far more than that of Tarquin his heart more cowardly in its lust than that of Iachmo , his intent deeper and his soul darker than Iago s his whole character so black , that if the combined ini- quity of Sodom and Gomorrah could be condensed boiled down, and then distilled into a quantity the size of his heart it would not be half so black so vile so devilish as that heart ! This is the character of the original of him whom we have taken as *our* Sam Selden   He is a true character as too many of our readers know especially ladies, for he is ever on the fashionable promenades and if he observes a lady whose beauty or manner strikes him he is sure to follow and annoy her   We have given his description before but it will be no harm to renew it   He is of middle size, slim well made, always *genteelly* dressed , wears a jet black beard and moustache, has very white teeth, which he is very fond of showing, a high, fair brow, a little overhanging his large, jet black eyes His complexion is pale, his manner calm and dignified

Fair readers this description is given for your benefit We know we have made out this man handsome—he is so—the serpent which seducing Eve from her duty to God and her husband brought misery and wretchedness into the world was also beautiful

This villain is a snake—you can see it in his fiery eyes, as such beware of him for we have given his exact description

So much for him—the assassin, gambler and libertine We will now resume the thread of our story When Carlton begged him to go on saying that he was calm Selden replied

' I will not say a word without you will promise me two things !

' What are they ?"

" The first is that you will offer no harm to your wife, what ever her conduct may have been !

" Well the second ?" cried the other impatiently

" That you never will tell her that I had anything to do with informing you !"

" Leave me the first out—the second I will agree to, willingly !"

" No Carlton both or neither !'

" Then both let it be Now go on, and tell me all !"

" You will offer her no violence ? '

" No—no ! I have said I would *not*—that is enough !"

" Yes for your word is better than your bond to a friend !"

" Well—well go on tell me all ! Is she false to me ?" cried Carlton, his voice trembling with agitation

" She told you that she had not been out for ten days ?"

" Yes this very morning she said so !"

" Then on this very morning she told a lie Night before last, you went out early to see some of your friends, did you not ?"

" Yes I did I believe !"

" You told her you could not spend the evening with her, that you had business which would keep you out till it was time for the bank to open ?"

Yes but how did you know that ?

You told me !

Ah did I ?   Well go on I had forgotten !"

' You went out   you had not been gone twenty minutes when I saw a female come down stairs   She was dressed very commonly had on your servant s cloak and bonnet and a thick green veil   I thought that she didn t look quite so tall as Eliza and as I had nothing to do before the bank opened I thought I d take a walk and see who it was that kept her face veiled so close !"

' Well well—go on tell me all !   Was it she ?   cried Carlton becoming more and more excited

' Just keep cool and you shall hear !   replied Selden deliberately pouring out a glass of wine and swallowing it (the wine not the glass)

He then continued

' I found she hurried on up Broadway so I took the other side and kept even with her careful all the time not to lose sight of her   We went on in this way until we got up to Leonard street where she turned to cross over to the right hand side of Broadway   I slunk back into the shade of the houses and she didn t see me and then as she passed on I followed   Before she had gone ten steps further she was met by a man who had evidently been waiting for her and taking his arm walked on up the street

But who was this woman—was this my wife ?   cried Carlton, now excited almost beyond the control of his resolution

Be calm my friend   be calm as you promised and hear all ! I *will* have my own way of telling this story !   replied Selden

And then he continued

When I saw this I shifted over to the other side of the street, and walked on——

" Did you know who the man was ?" asked Carlton

Yes   I recognized him by the light of the lamp that stands in front of one of the five story brick boarding houses there !

" Well who is he ?

" Just let me tell my story my own way, if you *please* !' said

Selden, filling himself another glass of wine and drinking it leisurely

"Well go on—go on ! You seem to take your time about it !"

"Yes I generally do in everything,' replied the villain, and then he continued his story

I kept on up the street a very little further back on the other side until we got to Canal street and here I saw they were about to cross over While they waited for a chance for some passing omnibuses kept them back I crossed over Canal and standing close in the shade of the brick store at the corner watched them till they crossed over and passed me, keeping down along the north side of Canal

I followed now at about ten or fifteen steps distance keeping close in the shade of the houses, and wrapping my large Spanish cloak close up around my face They kept on until they had got to ——— * street here they paused at the corner and the lady after a few words passed on to the next street The man, as soon as she had gone on went up the west side of —— street a few doors and stopping before the door of a three story brick house rung the bell He was admitted I then knew why the lady had gone on there was a back entrance to the same house !"

Yes it was Madame ——— s but the woman *was* she my wife ?

Wait till the time comes I tell you !' replied Selden 'hear the story my own way or don t hear it at all !

'Well go on for God's sake go on I m half crazy!

The Iago first poured out another glass of wine then after drinking it continued

"When I was fully satisfied of the drift of the game and saw the man whom I spotted and *knew* go into this assignation house I resolved to see who the woman was for as yet I had not made up my mind about her though I had my misgivings !

Well go on do make haste! cried Carlton nervously

Plenty of time—plenty of time! don t get yourself into a fret !' replied Selden

The author begs the reader s pardon for using these blanks in place of names but in these cases he is using information acquired in *confidence* " and he cannot be more explicit honorably

"I'm not fretting but, go on   You take things as easy as if you were preaching me a sermon !"

Selden continued

Therefore to make sure who she was, I went around to the back entrance and took a station in the shade opposite to it, across the street and waited

After I had been there about an hour the same woman came out   I followed her and at the very corner where they had separated he joined her again   I followed them on, and both of them kept on down Broadway till they got here to your very door and then he parted with her in the entry way, and here, for the first time, by the hall lamp, I got a sight of her face as she pulled aside her veil to kiss him !"

' And she was ——— '

" Your wife !'

"Great God I thought so ! I was sure of it—but she shall die ! I have forgiven before, but ———"

'Stop my friend, stop !" cried Selden laying his hand gently on the shoulder of the infuriated and almost raving Carlton "You promised to do her no harm !

' So I did but I made no promise in regard to *him !* Who is he ? Tell me and I ll have his heart's blood before I sleep !"

' Then I wont tell you   If you *will* act like a mad man, what is the use of my siding with you ?   I ll never tell you his name if you act in this way !"

"Sam is this your friendship ? Would you have me tamely submit to this insult this infernal wrong ?"

No of course not   But I d have you get your revenge safely and surely !'

"Well so you saw her kiss him and she was my wife !"

" Yes—and as I had satisfied himself on that point, I determined at first to put him out of the way   As I had no tools with me though I do generally carry them, I went up stairs to get a brace of pistols or the knife that I used up at the garden that night, you know   While I was gone, he cleared out, home, I supposed or up to his place   Well, I followed up there and looked in, but he wasn't there   So I went around to his boarding house and waited for him   Once I thought I had him but it turned out to be somebody else   and after all the fellow got clear !"

'Well you ll tell me who he is now ?   I m calm as ever I was! said Carlton

Yes, I'll tell you, if you ll promise to act only with me and on my advice !

' I will   for so far you have proved a good friend !"

" Then it is Charles Cooly !

" What ! Cooly—he whose place is in Broadway close to Leonard ?"

' Yes the same fellow !'

' Holy Heaven ! this is too much ! I could have borne it if she had picked out a man my superior in either looks feelings or any thing   But *he* !   He is not fit for a street sweeper   Why should she a woman with beauty education talent and wit, take up with such a clod hopping scoundrel as he ?

' There s no accounting for taste ! replied Selden in a dry tone

No there is not   but this fellow shall pay for his fun with his life !

Remember your promises   don't let her dream of anything, and do what you do in a way that'll keep you clear of the law ! said Selden

" Don t fear Sam the worst of my temper is over now, I'll be calm !' replied Carlton

Yet he was mistaken   The worst of his anger was not over Anger is like fire put to good fuel   while it flames and smokes it makes a greater and fiercer show, but when the fuel is burn ed down into coals how much more intense is its heat how much greater its power

So noisy, flaming anger is seldom very dangerous   it is the calm, settled, vindictive kind which is most to be dreaded

22

CHAPTER XVI

EARLY on the morning succeeding the night when we last describ d the scenes connected with them Big Lize and Angelina started in search of a boarding house for the latter The young girl was very feeble and scarcely able to walk Her face was pale and thin a few weeks of suffering had made sad havoc with her beauty And yet she looked very interesting with her large mournful looking eyes and her beautiful hair, which had once more been dressed with care Her wardrobe had been much improved, too, with the aid of her cousin who despite her many faults was liberal and kind and she really looked quite decent though very ill

They had not far to look for a boarding house for signs denoting such are almost as thick here as lawyers shingles are in Philadelphia

Lize soon obtained an interview with the landlady and representing herself as a working girl at a house where they would not take boarders asked for board for Angelina, as a sickly cousin, who had just come in from the country

The story of Lize suited well with her looks, for she had dressed plainly that morning and had used neither paint pow der nor curls therefore when she had satisfied the landlady of her ability to pay *weekly in advance,* the bargain for a room and board was easily made

" I shall come to see my cousin every evening and if she gets any worse you must call a doctor I will always see the bills paid ! said Lize and now ma am, if you please, we'll see what kind of a room you ll give her !'

" Certainly Miss walk up stairs and see Three rooms vacant—two on the third one on the fourth floor—dollar less for that and as for doctors we ve six in the house regular boarders ! replied the voluble landlady, at the same time leading the way up stairs

" *Six* doctors '' repeated Lize in surprise—' Why what do you do with them all ?

' Eat 'em and sleep em—regular boarders '"

' Eat them ? asked Angelina in a timid tone, which implied a desire not to remain under a roof where they eat people

' That is we feed and lodge them ' replied the landlady

Yes, but six doctors in one house ' that beats me '" muttered Lize

Oh, they're young ones , they don t count much, and then they're such good company ' They tell such funny stories about ghosts and digging up bodies and dissecting, and all that, you can't think ' Why I don t know what my daughters would do if it wasn t for them ''

By this time the landlady had arrived at the third floor, and showed Angelina one of the rooms for hire and as it suited her very well Lize concluded the bargain making all the necessary stipulations in regard to fire, lights &c

' I ll have your trunk sent along soon, cousin ' said Lize, as soon as all was settled

' My trunk ? replied the poor girl, remembering that she had nothing in the world save what she stood in for those who had murdered her mother had taken the last rag

Yes cousin I will send it soon '' replied Lize then, as she bent down to kiss her, she whispered—' I ll get you one, dear Now hold your tongue, don't speak or the old woman ll s pect suthin '

Angelina returned her cousin s kiss warmly, and held her peace , but tears stood in both her eyes as the latter arose and bade her good bye

' Don t feel bad or lonesome child I ll see you again to night '" said Lize and then, before the young girl could say another word the woman turned away with the landlady and Angelina was again alone

Oh how lonely she did feel when that door closed upon her ' She felt that she had but one friend in the world and that friend, who had twice protected her when in dark danger who had buried her mother, opened her purse to her, met her with every

Christian kindness was a courtesan a street walker, a panel thief!

And she was glad to have found such a protector—grateful to God for it for she knelt down when she was alone and thanked Him for His protection—and more she prayed that soon, very soon she might be permitted to follow her mother to that world where sorrow is not and trouble cannot come   Was she wrong in this? was that young helpless poor yet pure girl, wrong to pray God to remove her from this infectious world of sin and rottenness ere yet its foul disease had settled within her heart?

We will not say but let others think as they will

The first thing which Lize did after leaving her young cousin's room was to give more orders regarding her comfort to the land lady

She's a poor sickly thing said she ' and must be nursed careful!'

"She shall—I'll treat her just like one of my own daughters!" replied the landlady   She does look sickly—poor thing and just as if she'd been a crying for a week '

She has her mother died a few days ago! replied Lize

What of?   No catching disease I hope?

'Oh no, ma'am it was very sudden a kind of a strangulation or somethin !'

Oh yes what one of our doctors calls a ——"

"I haven't time to stop ma am! I must hurry home!' said Lize and so she escaped hearing the technical name for strangulation

She hurried away at once to a ready made dress store, and having taken Angelina's measure before they went out in the morning she soon purchased a quantity of new clothing which she knew would fit her tolerably well and do it any rate, until she could have her fitted out better by a regular dress maker Purchasing a trunk she paid the bill and ordered her purchase sent home   She then made many other little purchases such as articles for the toilet shoes stockings &c and soon had every thing which the poor girl *needed* and many little articles of lux ury beside

After getting home, and packing all the things she nailed a neat card upon the trunk, on which she had written the name,

" Miss Angelina Lindsay ' and paying a porter, bade him carry the trunk to the house where she had left her cousin

'Be careful not to say where you took the trunk from, just leave it ask and answer no questions and when you come back, I'll give you another quarter!'

Thank ye ma am it s myself, Dinnis O Flaherty as 'll do yer biddin ony day for sich bright looks an good quarthers! replied the por er, hurrying off with his load But he had not gone ten steps from the door, when he heard himself called back

I forgot to send the key The young lady would be troubled to open it without that said Lize at the same time handing the key to the porter

" Yes sure would she ma am widout she was an ould young un!' replied the man

Lize did not exactly like his looks and as she had nothing better to do she said, It s no matter! give me the key—I ll go around with you!

'Och, very well ma am—but, about the other quarther—if you go wid me you won t be here to give it to me as you said you would, whin I come back!

It s all the same—I ll give it to you there! replied Lize and now the porter started off with her close behind him

In twenty minutes more the trunk was in Angelina's room, and the key in her possession

Woman *always* has curiosity, so had Angelina and the con tents of the trunk were soon looked over The dresses and little articles of fancy were looked at carelessly but one of her kind cousin s purchases was taken up, looked at first with sur prise then with pleasure, and pressed to the young girl s lips fondly and fervently

Methinks I hear my readers wonder what present a fallen wretched and degraded courtesan could have selected which should so p'ease a pure and good girl Many a guess would they make I think before they would touch the right object but we'll save them the trouble of wondering It was a *Bible* If Lize was not good herself she knew of the book which good people do love—and she judged rightly that it would be an ac ceptable present for her young cousin

After Angelina had examined her trunk she took her new Bible in her hand and went to her window and seated herself by it   The day was beautiful out   and though it was winter still the sun shone mildly down upon the house tops, making even the snow look warm and sweaty

She could not refrain from raising her window   As she did so and gazed out looking up and down the street, the fresh air came and gave a little more color to her cheek

Suddenly however that color faded—her cheek became white as the snow on the opposite roof and as she drew her head quickly in she gasped and murmured

Again—again ! Oh God help me—my persecutor again !'

Then she peeped carefully from the window once more and as she did so quickly again drew back, and murmured

'He stops at this door—oh, God ! Have I been betrayed—*who* could have sent him here !

She paused a moment as if for thought and to gather strength, and then she cried

I will fly—I will not stay here—he shall insult me no more !'

In one moment more she had put on her bonnet and shawl her veil was doubled over her face, and leaving her trunk open everything just as it was when she opened the window she hurried from the room

When she had passed down the stairs and reached the front door a gentlemen was just entering the parlor and in his voice she recognized *Livingston*   It was him whom she had seen from her window and yet he did not come there to seek her, nor did he dream of her vicinity when she passed him and went out

This was the house of Mrs Windeman   Livingston had called to see Maria Deloraine who still retained her rooms here, though to excuse her temporary residence at Madame I s she pretended to be on a visit to a sick friend   Yet at certain hours she managed to be   at home   to meet sundry little engagements

Had Angelina known all this she would not again have been a homeless wanderer in the street but alas she *was !*

CHAPTER XVII

On the evening of the same day when Carlton advanced him the money Meadows began his dreadful servitude by furnishing him with impressions of every important key in his employer s store This Carlton had demanded in a note which he wrote him but an hour afterward and as Charles had charge of the keys, this was an easy thing for him to do especially as directions how to procure the impressions were given

As we have already seen after this was done he staggered home pale weak and almost fainting from the effects of the dreadful excitement through which he had passed on that day

He had not been home long when Harry Whitmore returned with a carriage to convey Isabella as both she and her mother supposed to his sister s on a visit

It was strange that neither brother or mother felt any sus picion or wondered why he should take her away just at night fall but they did not for the conduct of Whitmore before the females had been very pure and exemplary and the brother only thought him a little wild and even conceived that this was caused by his over good heartedness

And Isabella went with a heart half sad and yet glad She scarcely knew how to feel As the hour approached—she cer tainly felt more and more that natural fear which any pure and delicate maiden *must* feel but then she *loved* Whitmore and where woman loves she is *all* confidence She did not dream of deceit Yet when she parted with her mother, then her eyes were tearful and she kissed her with more than her usual fervor She went to her brother too and kissed his feverish brow with her moist warm lips and bade him good night with a trembling voice

Her mother responded to her parting words with a

" Good night God bless you, my dear child !' which thrilled to the bottom of the daughter's heart

"God bless her! Indeed did she then need His blessing and protection but Providence seemed to have abandoned her, pure and innocent as she was

Yet who shall dare to condemn the all wise and far seeing Creator for this who shall murmur at his will All things are ordered for the best and this though we cannot see its good must be connected with the great scheme of life and its neces sary changes

Isabella and her intended seducer entered the carriage which he had prepared and hurried away to Greenwich street

While they were leaving the carriage and standing before the door of Madame I another carriage drove rapidly past It was close curtained and had but one occupant yet she was one of our characters one who had a sad and heavy heart Her des tination too was a house in Greenwich street one of most "*un*-questionable character

Poor Mary Sheffield—she too had parted with her mother parted perchance never to see her again had received a blessing and a kiss as Isabella had but oh how differently was she situated

But she might have been only a little advanced in misery Was not the other on the verge of taking the same road which she had followed? Was Isabella more pure as she stood there while the carriage of Mary drove past than was Mary Sheffield five months before? No—alas no! What would five months more bring to Isabella Meadows? Alas who then could say?

———

True to her promise Big Lize called at Mrs Windeman's at night fall to see Angelina Upon inquiring for her she was told that she had gone out not more than an hour before dinner and had not since returned

Lize hurried up to her room where she found everything in confusion just as the poor frightened girl had left it her Bible laying on the chair by the window—the window still open

My God!" murmured the woman, 'what can have become of her?'

I can't tell—can't imagine ' said Mrs Windeman, who had also come up stairs, the servant girl saw her go out '"

She went alone, didn t she ? ' asked Lize

"Yes but she seemed in a great hurry and all of a tremble like the girl noticed it particularly, for she d just let in a gen tleman '

' A *gentleman* ? Did he speak to her ? '

No he didn t come to see her he came to visit one of my boarders, Miss Deloraine '"

' Who was he—do you know him ? '

Oh yes he s a particular friend of Aramintina one of my daughters He s the rich handsome Mr Gus Livingston '

Gus Livingston ? muttered Lize, I ve heard that name before '

Yes, I dare say you have everybody knows him—he's so rich and so handsome They do say he pays particular atten tion to Miss Deloraine but my Aramintina says it s no such thing, and she had it from his own lips ' '

"Livingston ? Gus Livingston ? Oh yes by heaven ' I re member now I see it all the poor gal saw him a comin when she looked out of the window and then she cut and run ' cried Lize who had not heeded the remarks of the landlady

She seemed almost maddened with the thought '

Where on earth could she be ? murmured she again then while anger flushed her face and brightened her eye she cried

' Curse that Livingston ' If harm befalls that poor gal I ll have his heart s blood '

' Oh *my* ! how you *do* talk ' Why he had nothing to do with her '"

' You lie, you old hag ' I tell you he had ' He drove her out of your rotten old crib here '

' Hag ? how dare you talk so to me ' I thought you wasn't any better than you should be ' screamed the angry landlady

Out of my way afore I walk right over you ' I m a goin to look for the gal and if I don t find her you and your Gus Livingston shall suffer or my name s not Big Lize ' that s all git out of the way ' shouted the enraged woman and pushing Mrs W aside she sprang down the stairs and hurried away

Her first idea was to search for Angelina but she knew that she might nearly as well look for a needle in a haystack as to try to seek out the poor girl in this vast city without some trace of her route and she then determined to meet her pal as she had promised in Thomas street, and to get his aid as well as that of all the prowling gang, who being ever on the walk might stand some chance of finding her out

She therefore hurried on up Greenwich street and had nearly reached the corner where she would turn up toward Broadway when the door of a carriage which had just stopped close before a door which she was passing opened, and a gentleman stepped out of it muffled in a cloak   She got a glimpse of his face as he stepped on the pavement, for there were lights attached to the carriage and she at once recognized a man whom she had twice knocked down

It was Livingston

"Curse you ! I have found you have I !" she cried springing upon him and clenching him by the throat,   Where is the gal ?"

Stop stop my good woman you are making a mistake !" cried Livingston   I am a minister !" and as he said this he dropped his cloak and showed that he was robed in the full cos tume of a clergyman

But she had seen his face and she knew it well

Minister be d——d ! she cried   I know you, Gus Living ston ! I d know you in any rig !

Livingston was naturally a coward, but his present business made him doubly so and while his whole frame trembled he cried

Let go of me my good woman ! Let go of me—I tell you you are mistaken ! Here, take my purse   there s nearly fifty dollars in it ! take it and let me go !"

D——n your money ! Where s the gal ?' shrieked the wo man, clenching him still closer and beginning to choke him

In the house I s pose !" gasped the terrified villain

The woman dashed him to the earth with terrific force where he lay amid a crowd, which was rapidly collecting, and as she did so, turned to the door, which at that moment was opened by a gentleman for the noise made had already alarmed the neigh borhood

What is the matter here? What the h—l is the row?" asked this gentleman as he stepped out upon the threshold

'Go to h—l and see! shouted Lize madly for in Whitmore she recognised another of those who had insulted her cousin be fore Florence s and as she spoke she dashed his head violently against the door post and rushed into the house

Turning into the open parlor, she saw three females, all of them apparently much terrified

Where is the gal? Give her up, you bloody strumpets or I ll tear the house down !

'Oh mercy the woman is mad ! murmured Isabella for there she stood dressed all in white ready for the bridal

What do you want?" asked Maria Deloraine and Miss Wood who were more calm because perchance they were more used to such scenes

My cousin ! my poor cousin ! She s here I know she is, for I ve seen the men that tried to take her off before Blast em I ve given em sore heads for one while ! cried Lize

Woman you re crazy Go away or we ll call the police ! said Maria advancing toward her

Call your police if you dare ! They re just the people I want I know what kind of a house this is Give up my cousin, or I ll call the police !

'Who is your cousin? she cannot be here ! said Isabella, tim idly for she had begun to recover a little from her fright

Lize looked at her before she spoke and that glance deter mined her answer

Look ee Miss you looks as if you was innocent like and hadn t been long in such a house as this do tell me where they ve hid my poor cousin ?

Maria saw by the look of Isabella that she began to be alarmed and placed herself at once between her and the woman

Don t listen to her, dear sister ! she cried The woman is certainly crazy !

"No not crazy yet ! replied Lize more calmly but I soon

shall be if I don t find poor Angelini   Oh for God's sake give her up to me !"

Isabella was touched by the imploring tone of the woman and despite her alarm, saw that something must be wrong and determined to become satisfied

Who is Angelina?   she asked, coming forward and looking Lize in the face

She is my cousin Miss—a young innocent girl—one that looks as pure as you do who I m sure ought never to have come to a house like this !

Like this?   What do you know of this house ?

What   don t you know—are you not yet a victim ?

A victim?   To what?   Tell me quickly !

Maria saw that this would not do   exposure was but too cer tain if it continued and she cried

Isabella you must not listen to this woman she is crazy come do come into the back room !

Miss Wood too joined in pressing her to leave the room but so far forgot herself as to use some very coarse epithets toward Lize

How it would have ended now we know not but the entrance of two more persons on the scene made an instant change

Isabella saw her affianced lover stagger in the room his face covered with blood supported by a man garbed as a minister whose nose was also bleeding

What is the matter, Henry?   Oh mercy !   What *is* the matter ?   she shrieked

"Nothin Miss, only I mashed his head a little agin the wall, for him and that other scoundrel have stolen my cousin !"

'D—n that woman she is always in our way ! cried Liv ingston forgetting his clerical robe

Isabella heard this and turning to Lize said

Do you know that man—is he not a minister ?

One of the devil s ministers Miss   He is Gus Livingston, one of the wildest rakes in town !"

Water—water murmured Whitmore   I shall faint !   As he said this he staggered to a sofa and fell back on it   But Isabella did not move to help him

She stood like one spell bound   With her hands clasped ove
her brow as if to keep her head from bursting with the dread
ful thought which had entered it she stood and looked first at
one and then another of the party

Maria self convicted had sunk down upon a chair and burst
into tears   Emma Wood alone had the presence of mind to go
for water for Whitmore, who had indeed fainted

Livingston stood by the door as if he intended to run away
looking both frightened and foolish

This lasted only a second   It was broken by Lize who made
a bound upon Livingston and before he could move seized him
by the neck

"Where is my cousin? she shrieked   Give her up or by the
God that made you I ll choke you to death! what are you a
doin here with a priest's gown upon you?"

Let go of me good woman—don t go to raise such a cursed
row here! I don t know your cousin!"

Take that for lyin you blasted thief! shouted Lize giving
him a cuff upon the ear which would have knocked him down
if she had not upheld him with the other hand

D——n you, let me go! cried Gus maddened by the pain
and striking her heavily

"That s your game is it my covey!' cried the strong woman
"Two can play at it then!'

As she said this with her clenched hand she struck him two
tremendous blows, which left him completely senseless   The
next moment when she let go of him with her left hand he fell
limberly to the floor and made no motion to get up

' Lay there, you worthless dog!" cried Lize spurning him with
her foot

She now advanced to Isabella, and with a changed tone and
manner begged her to tell her where they had hidden poor An
gelina

I know nothing woman, indeed I do not,' she replied   "Oh
God what can all this mean?"

She then turned to Maria who having lost all self command
was weeping in the corner and said,

"Maria, there is something very wrong here! oh as you are

a woman tell me—tell me if you love me ! and the beautiful girl knelt down before the courtesan

Go away from here—quick Leave the house before he comes too ! sobbed Maria— do—do—it is your only safety !"

'I will—I will—oh thank God I ve a home to go to ! shriek ed Isabella who though not yet comprehending all the plot, knew that she was in some imment danger

But as she turned to the door she saw that Whitmore had re covered through the aid of Emma and was once more on his feet

He sprang in an instant to the door—the key was on the in side He locked it and put the key in his pocket

Where were you going dear Isabella ? he asked

Home sir ! home to stay there until this strange mystery is explained !

Dearest—it—it can be explained on the spot, that woman is crazy !

Lize did not speak she stood over Livingston with her arms folded as if she was waiting for him to get up again

Isabella looked a moment at Whitmore, and then replied

' I do not care whether she is crazy or not ! I *will* go home !"

' Isabella replied he in a calm firm tone you shall not, until I have had a chance for explanation !"

Well sir go on explain quickly—is he a minister ? and she pointed to the prostrate Livingston

Yes certainly and ere this moment would have married us, had it not been for that crazy woman

Marriage in a house like this ! Talk of religion in hell and vice in heaven ! *Marriage* here ! Ha ! ha ! that *is* a joke ! cried Lize and then before another word could be ut ered by Whitmore she turned to Isabella and said

' Young woman I begin to see into this 'ere business That swell has brought you here on a promise to marry you and he's put this other cove up to *sham* minister He d have married you for a month and then have kicked you out o doors These here gals are no better than I and I've been on the town for years !

Shameless wretch ! cried Whitmore, " stop your lying ! Is- abella you can see she is crazy !

"Crazy or not Henry I wish to go home Once more I ask you to open the door !

"But you cannot go home without a carriage !"

"There is one at the door I saw it when I looked from the window a moment ago ! replied Isabella

I do not care Isabella you shall not go till I explain and satisfy you that nothing is wrong !

Do let her go Harry do let her go or I ll tell her all ! said Maria still sobbing and advancing to Whitmore

He saw how inopportune was this remark and in a moment, maddened by anger struck her heavily on the face crying—

Take that for your interference !

She tottered back and fell to the floor while the red blood gushed from her mouth

'Oh coward ! how *could* you strike your sister ! cried Isabella indignantly

'I m not his *sister !* Oh save yourself while you can !" murmured Maria and then fainted

Emma Wood who had stood idly by not knowing what to do sprung to her, and now exclaiming—

You re no man Harry Whitmore to strike a woman ! I ll have nothing more to do with your infernal villainy !

Give me the key of that door ! I will not stay longer ! I now begin to see it all ! cried Isabella

If you do Miss then you shall stay and see it through ! replied Whitmore now boldly throwing off even the guise of affection You shall not leave this house to night You came here with your own consent—you shall only leave it with mine !

Oh mercy ! God of heaven protect me ! murmured the helpless girl Henry Whitmore if you have a man s heart in you let me go ! I will forgive all you have intended, only do, pray let me go !"

'I will when I get ready but not to night Why girl, you re foolish ! this is our wedding night !

'No no ! That night never will come ! I will die before you shall ever be husband to me ! '

"Well, well just as you like ! If you won t *marry* me I assure you I shall not press the matter, but you are mine now !"

Oh God ! never ! never ! Is there no way of getting out of this terrible place ?' screamed the unhappy girl

Yes gal there is and I ll help you ! replied Lize, stepping to the window and flinging up the sash

As she did this her shrill voice rung along the street and she screamed—

Watch ! Watch ! Murder ! Help ! Help !'

Whitmore knew the effect which this cry would have and raising Isabella in his arms before she could move he sprung through the back parlor doors and disappeared

Twice her scream was heard—wild loud and fearful and then all was still—still as the grave

When Lize heard the hurrying footsteps of the watchmen, she turned again to the room and saw that Whitmore and Isabella had disappeared but Livingston had regained his feet

Emma Wood had been busy in trying to recover poor Maria —so far without success

At this moment Whitmore returned and putting in the key at once opened the door

"Where is the girl ? asked Livingston in a whisper

' Safe in the cellar tied and gagged !' replied Whitmore, in the same tone   Now support me and we ll soon have this noisy lady hushed up   She shall see that the watch is called to some purpose or I m mistaken   Here Emma take Maria into the back parlor   Gus help her quick !   Then shut and lock the door

This was done and when Whitmore opened the front door to the watchmen who came, there was no one but Big Lize and Livingston in the front parlor   The carriage which Livingston came in but had forgotten to pay drove off at the first alarm

"What s the divilmint ? asked one of the watchmen his brogue betraying that he was Irish like nearly one half or per haps more of his brethren   in office

"There's one of the women in the house crazy drunk, and she s been fighting and raising a row   I wish you'd take care of her !'

"Faith that we will!" replied the other, and the two followed Whitmore into the parlor

'Which is the crater?" asked the first watchman as he entered, for both Livingston and Lize were particularly quiet at that moment

"There—the woman, seize her—she has raised the row!"

Lize, who had been struck dumb by the sudden disappearance and quiet of Isabella, had stood wondering what had become of her but now she spoke

"Are you watchmen?" she asked of the guardians of the night

"Faith, that we are, so come along wid us pacably like a lady, now!" said No 1, shaking his large club most uninvitingly

'Then do your duty! Arrest those men! for I believe there's been a murder done here within less than five minutes past!"

"A murder! Just hear her! Why she just broke in and tried to murder us! Look how we're bleeding yet!"

'So they are! and she looks big enough to ate 'em up!" replied watchee No 2

"Come along wid us, we knows you!" said No 1

'But, it is not me that you want, it was I that called you, these young men have a young woman in the house, that they're trying to ruin, and——"

"Just hear her! I told you she was crazy, or drunk!" cried Whitmore, and Livingston added

"Yes she's undoubtedly crazy Do take her off, my good fellows There's an X for your trouble!'

"Sure, an it's no trouble at all, at all your honor!" said No 2, pocketing the ten dollar note, at the same time, saying,

"I'll halve it wid ye, Phalim, when we git it changed!"

'Well, come along wid ye," cried the other to Lize, 'if ye called us, ye wanted us, sure, and here we are arter you!"

'You will not arrest those villains, then?" asked Lize "Sure an I don't see ony, 'ceptin' it be yourself!" replied No 2, and as they both began to sidle up toward her, No 1, said

'Now, behave yourself like a dacent woman, as may be ye are, an can prove to his honor in the mornin', do now, an' come along wid us, like a lady!"

23

"Keep back keep back ! I will not be arrested !" cried she, and, quick as lightning, she snatched the large club from the speaker's hand

The other watchman struck at her, but she met his blow and before he could again raise his hand, she struck him down   The other sprang to his aid, and shared the same fate   The coast was nearly clear now and Lize sprung through the open door, dashed through the crowd, which had been gathered in the street, by the noise, and in a moment more was safe having turned up a dark and narrow alley, which led out of the main thorough fare

"Be jabers but she did hit hard ! ' muttered watchman, No 1 about three minutes after she had left picking himself up at the same time

" Sure an I think it was a man in gals petticoats, I do !" mut tered the other, rubbing his head

Where is the divil ?" asked No 1

"She s clear she ran out of the door !" replied Whitmore

"Och, yer honer why didn't yez knock her down ?'

"She had your cudgel in her hand and seemed inclined to do all the knocking herself, but, never mind let her go now !' re plied Whitmore who was glad enough to be rid of her, and wished now to have the watchmen leave also

Yis ' replied No 1   we may as well agree to let her go now, for she has taken the *lave* whither or no   But she said some thing about murder !'

"Oh, she was crazy, I told you, ' replied Whitmore, " here is another X for you, to save your friend the trouble of changing his !'

"Ah, thank yer honer , we ll drink your health wid it !'

' Very well good night !"

"Good night yer honers, pleasant dreams wid ye !'

The watchmen went away   Whitmore and Livingston were once more alone

" Well by thunder this *was a go !*" muttered Livingston, who had divested himself of his clerical gown, when he assisted Em ma to take Maria to the back parlor

"But we're out of it ' Now you can take yourself home as soon as you like '

What, Harry ' sha n t I stay to marry you ?

No, blast it no ' I ll not even do her the honor of a *sham* marriage now   I shall not want you any more, but I'll be at your rooms in the morning '"

Early ?

' Can't say as to that   but wait there till I come '"

'Very well   good night '"

When Livingston had gone away Whitmore went into the back parlor

Maria had recovered from her fainting fit, and Emma was washing away the blood stains

' I am very sorry Maria that I struck you " said he, in a contrite tone   but you made me so angry that I didn t know what I was about '

Where is Isabella ? asked Maria, not heeding his apology

Gone home she s safe , but don't be angry with me ' replied Whitmore, "I did not know what I was about, when I struck you '"

' No you did not but I can tell you   You was making for yourself the bitterest foe' that ever followed a man to curse him ' You have *lied* to me   Isabella Meadows is in the house Emma saw you carry her back when I lay senseless where you had laid me with a mean, unmanly blow '

Maria, I took her to the back door and let her go, so that she should not tell the watchmen   The moment I let her go she ran through to the street and as the watchmen came in I saw her go up toward her home '"

While Whitmore spoke, Maria gazed him steadily in the eye but he was enough of an accomplished villain to bear all this and returned her gaze without a flush or tremor

' You may speak truth and you may not Harry Whitmore, but if you do wrong that poor girl, may her curse, my curse and the curse of God Almighty rest upon you '"

Whitmore did blanch a little when he heard these words in a stern tone but he recovered himself in a moment, and said

I've given her up, Maria, you need not fear for her, but do make up with me!

'Never never sir! You struck me—a woman, even as if I had been a beast!

'But Maria you blinded me with anger!"

"I care not—there is no excuse for a man raising his hand to a woman Would to God the arm that is raised to strike any woman, if it be the hand of a man, could be blasted ere it fell!'

'Well, well Maria if you will quarrel with me you must But I don't deserve it!'

Don't deserve it? Does a murderer deserve hanging?'

Whitmore did not reply immediately—but commenced counting some money from his pocket book After he did so he passed a small roll of notes toward Maria, saying

There are the thousand dollars Miss Deloraine If your part of the bargain is not fulfilled, *mine* shall be!"

Maria was evidently touched at this apparent generosity but she neither spoke or reached out her hand to receive the money

Whitmore then laid it in her lap and taking out two fifty dollar notes from his pocket book handed it to Miss Wood

"There Emma take that—I'm sorry I've given you so much trouble Now, ladies, I'll bid you good evening!"

He turned away as if he really meant to leave the house—and this at once caused Maria to think that Isabella had indeed gone home

'Stop a moment, Mr Whitmore," said she "where were you going?'

"To my lodgings Miss Deloraine,—have you any command?"

No, sir—but—but I do not think it right for me to take your money Have the kindness to take it back!

'No you said some time ago that you needed just one thousand dollars, that with it you could accomplish some purpose which you had long cherished Keep it, and may you be happy!"

His tone was now kind though cold, and as it was assumed on purpose to deceive her and to work upon her better feelings, it succeeded

Emma kissed her, and said,

"Do make it up with Harry, Maria! I'm sure he is sorry he struck you !

Indeed, I am !' added Whitmore

Maria whose heart was of a strange compound a mixture of good and bad with both natures ever struggling to gain the ascendancy did not need this interference of Emma s to decide her   Her impulsive mind quick to anger and as quickly calm again had already changed, and she said

"I ll forgive you Harry—but even now I do not like to take this money ! You have failed in your undertaking, perhaps through me !"

' Never mind—keep the money   I've lost the girl but there are as good fish in the sea as ever were caught ! replied Harry at the same time drawing Emma Wood to him and impressing a kiss upon her full red lips

The girl seemed flattered by this attention and returned the kiss perhaps as a kind of receipt for the hundred dollars which he had given her

Maria thought that as affairs seemed to be turning, her com pany was not needed and rising said

I ll go home Harry now if you have no objections !"

"None in the world Maria if you have entirely forgiven me !

Oh yes and I will try to forget all but your kindness !" re plied the girl   'Give me a kiss Harry, and consider all made up !'

"Certainly Maria—I wish I could forgive myself as easily for that unlucky blow !'

' Don t think of it any more Harry—come and see me to morrow if you can for I shall leave town in a day or two !"

I will Maria ! Good night !   The girl left the room to get her cloak and bonnet and in a few moments more left the house

So much for her !" cried Whitmore after he heard the outer door slammed to and knew thereby that she had left   'So much for her she's out of the way !'

" Well what do you intend to do with yourself Harry ?"asked

Miss Wood, with a smile "You don't intend to go home to-night, oh?

'No indeed ' replied the libertine

"Then I suppose that——"

" You needn t suppose anything at all, Emma !" replied Whitmore interrupting her   you can retire as soon as you choose I do not need your company any more to night '"

"Why Harry how strange you talk ! I thought——'

Confound it ' I don t want you to think ! I want your room, not your company '"

' But Harry there is no one in the house but us   You know when Madame I gave it up for this affair to you, I was to re main in charge !

Yes you were and to let me do just as I pleased in the house !

That is true   now what do you please to do?   Will you have some wine?

'No I wish no wine   I want you to go to bed, and if you hear any noise to forget it, and pay no attention to it '"

' Then the girl is in the house yet?

To be sure she is !   Do you think I d let her slip after I d got her fairly in my hands?

It wouldn t have been much like vou, but what do you in tend now?

That is my business you go to bed, and to sleep   Here is another fifty put it under your pillow to dream upon '"

Thank you, Harry, but you are so wild I must pity the poor creature !

Pity her? Ha ! ha ! that is a good joke Emma from you How long is it since I heard you wish you had it in your power to bring all woman kind down to a level with your class !

'I believe I did say something like that, but then I didn t have a case like this right before me to think of !

Well well girl you may save your pity   She will never be any worse off than you are ! Now just become invisible as soon as possible, she must be half dead with cold and fright '"

' Where is she?

" In the cellar ! I laid her down on a pile of straw, or something '"

"She keeps very still may be she is dead '"

" No danger of that, she wont die so easy, but, as for her keeping quiet, you would too if you had a handkerchief stuffed in your mouth, and your hands and feet tied !"

Oh, how could you serve her so ! Harry you are cruel by Heaven, if you had treated me so, I'd kill you, if I had to be hung for it !'

I don t think you would ever put a man to such a necessity !" replied Harry with a smile, "but, leave me, I'm going down af ter her !'

Emma, who did not seem much pleased with his course, arose, and slowly left the room, while he hurried away to the cellar

In a moment more he hurried back to the parlor, for a light, muttering as he came

"She isn t where I laid her down ! curse it, how could she move when I bound her so tight !

He again descended and after a moment he rushed up the stairs, cursing and swearing at every step

" Emma ! Emma !' he shouted

"Well, what is it? asked the cyprian bending over the bal istrades of the stair way, for she now was in the second story

' The girl has escaped ! By thunder, this is too bad ! But she must be in the house !"

"I hope not' murmured the girl, "poor thing, how I pity her !"

This was said as Whitmore commenced a search in the lower rooms At the moment when she expressed her pity, Emma heard a noise behind her, and, even before she could turn, heard a low moan and the words—

"Oh, save me ! save me ! For the love of heaven, save me !"

She looked around, and there stood poor Isabella—her white dress stained with the earth of the cellar—her face pale as mar ble—her eyes wild with terror—her whole frame quivering with the agony of fear

"Oh save me save me !' murmured the poor girl, kneeling— her hands clasped together, and great tears standing in her large eyes

"I will, if I can ! Oh where can I put you ! He will search the house There—go in my room ! Hide under the bed !

Don't move, or hardly breathe ! I'll do all I can for you—poor, poor girl !'

As Isabella hurried into the room of Emma, the steps of Whitmore were heard   He was already ascending the stairs, having sought in vain for his unfortunate victim below   He appeared to be in a fearful rage,—curses, bitter and loud, were on his lips, coupled with such threats as made even Emma Wood tremble

END OF PART THREE.

APPENDIX

APPENDIX

WE have some remarks to make to our readers, which properly would have belonged in the Preface but as that happens already to be in print, we have no other choice than to place them here

During the progress of this work many of our friends have evinced a very kind anxiety for its success and its good character and as all of these have had various suggestions to make it is but justice to them to take some notice of their various hints and we doubt not, well meant advice

One says, " don't put so much slang into your thieves mouths !" Another tells us that we have permitted the blank 'd——n' to be seen in one or two cases in the work another says we make our descriptions too horrible another wants still other alterations

To one and all we give this answer

This book is intended to be a *mirror of life* as it is in this city we are guided entirely by life as we have seen it here, and *will* be natural and true to that life We will put such language into the mouths of our characters as their originals really use—a thief speaks in the thief tongue and he scarcely knows any other We pride ourself not so much on making this a pretty or an interesting *novel* as we do in giving *true* pictures of our characters We would like to please every one—but those who cannot be pleased with this must go displeased

While we have been annoyed by anonymous and cowardly letters from gamblers and other *things* of the same species, we have received many others from all parts of the Union which much encourages us in our duty and one which we regret is anonymous (for the writer appears to be a good and philosophical man, one whom we should like to know,) we here insert

HUDSON, Feb 12 1848

" SIR —Having read with infinite satisfaction your first numbers of the Mysteries and Miseries of New York I cannot but conclude that if the Mirror is held up faithfully to nature it reflects most powerfully on Vice its true image and character   The representations of misery which are certainly confirmed by the authority of one of our most zealous and able magistrates as well as by your own offers to those whose chivalry or philanthropy might over rule their scruples would appear almost in credible even to a citizen of the World who might not have had an op portunity to learn that such things actually are have been and are likely to continue

Will you allow then one of those Strangers to observe that it would be a matter of serious consideration and highly important to your readers that the *census* of the City should be introduced with its several *distinc tions numbers complexions houses grades*—to ascertain this even in your spirit of adventure would be a matter of inquiry from *authority* attended with little difficulty

In a letter of the very eccentric Wm Cobbett to the people of Botley dated North Hempstead L Island Nov 10 1818 he makes this singular remark   'However the best proof of the inutility of an established church is the absence of crimes in this country compared to the state of England in that respect   There has not been three felonies tried in this county since I arrived in it   The Court House is two miles from me An Irishman was tried for forgery in the summer of 1817 and the whole county was alive to go and witness the novelty   I have not heard of a man being hanged in the United States since my arrival   The Boroughmongers in answer to statements like these say that this is a thinly inhabitated country   This very county is more thickly settled than Hampshire   The adjoining county towards the City of New York is much more thickly settled than Hampshire   *New York itself contains nearly two hundred thousand inhabitants* and after London is the first com mercial and maritime city in the world —Thousands of sailors ship carpenters dock yard people cartmen draymen boatmen &c crowd its wharfs and quays   Yet never do we hear of a hanging *scarcely ever of a robbery   men go to bed with scarcely locking their doors   and never is seen in those streets what is called in England a girl of the town and what is still more never is there seen in those streets a beggar   I wish* you my old neighbors could see this City of New York   (Copy)

' Amen say I I wish they could perhaps even nowadays they would not see *a beggar* such a character falling immediately under the eye of the Police—but this statement of Wm Cobbett has of course been uni versally read and in the present aspect of our modern Utopia forms a strange contrast with the fearfulness of your pages

" I have been induced to make these remarks the more particularly from

reasons that our foreign relations whilst they justly appreciate the mea
sure of our importance and civilization have not reflected till lately on
the progress of our attainments   Philosophy will tell us that there can
be refinement in Vice more aptly than in Virtue   Sero Nostri says
Cicero, literas didicere at recepta ab aliis fecere meliora a quibus didi
cerunt   Your Book will teach *how much* we have both *borrowed and im
proved* and what is by the Roman orator applied to Literature is equally
notorious by developments of Ingenuity in us both natural and acquired
Under these circumstances it is but right that those who would profit by
our wisdom should understand *from what causes under what auspices* we are
becoming a model or serving as a moral to mankind—for that mankind
will be indebted to you for your fortitude and exertions I have no doubt.

   Permit me to subscribe myself your sincere admirer with every wish
for your success in your undertaking

                              " Respectfully   L "

   Our correspondent is in error so far as regards the not *seeing*
a beggar" in our streets   They are almost as thick as the hogs
are and especially about our large hotels are hundreds of them
daily seen ragged, filthy and disgusting   But these are not the
really needy ones—they are *professional* beggars   The *poor*
people are too sick and naked generally to get out
   But to the other portions of our unknown correspondents
letter   He quotes from a letter of Wm Cobbett which may
have truth in it or may not for Cobbett like most great men,
was very prejudiced   We have endeavored to find this letter
so as to compare it with others from the same author but in a
hasty glance over his works we have missed it nor have we
time with this number to look it up *   Will our friend have
the kindness to tell us where we can find it in print?   It was origi
nally and is still our intention to furnish in an Appendix to this
work the very information which our correspondent asks and
also to contrast the present state of the city with its past con
dition and to institute so far as our poor powers will enable
us a strict inquiry into the causes of the great change which
certainly has taken place within a few years, and is now mak
ing daily more fearful progress
   The writer cannot lay all of the disgusting immoralities of
this city before his readers—he can only say that it is now bid

---

* If it is in his   Year's residence in America   we have been unable to procure
the book in time to read it before our issue of this number

ding fair to out rival Paris in its obscenity and vice The taste runs but too much for "model artists ' dog fights and the like , and the crowded state of our prisons prove that there is indeed some change between the time of Cobbett and this, if he spoke truly

We are sickened with the details which are before us—we are heartily sickened with the task which we have undertaken, but, we will not now turn back We will point out the things we see at least such as will bear writing of, and if the citizens and their servants, the city authorities, who are *paid* to protect them and the credit of the town, will do their duty much good can soon be accomplished

The gambling houses ought to be, and *can* be broken up As we have said before gaming is carried on *openly* every night in some places in broad day light In Reed street, not twenty steps from Broadway is a den where more than one man has had his cash "*exchanged* and seen his *peck* of trouble" and here a faro bank is open day and night Is this so secret that the guardians of the insulted law cannot find it?

Let any one whose *duty* it is to put a stop to such work, go to a certain No 54 in that neighborhood and see if the law is either feared or respected

Again we ask for what purpose is the second floor of the house 564 Broadway used? Let those whose duty it is go and see and they may become acquainted with very many of our most *fashionable* young men—the scions of our aristocracy—the hopeful members of the rising generation—those who are here after to sustain the credit and places of their fathers

We do hope that the City Council which lately has so proper ly taken in hand the 'model artist system, will also look into the gambling shops—for while the exhibition of nude women ex cites the licentious passions of our young men—gambling ex cites and encourages every bad passion of the human heart Envy avarice stealing intemperance, revenge, lying, deceit— even murder ! We may offend many by coming out thus plain ly and giving locations—but we care not we have declared a war against these wretches, and if we live, we will treat them worse than ever ' Rough and Ready" did the Mexicans.

There are many other things which we wish to notice, but

There are many other things which we wish to notice but have not room for them in this No of our work Our next part will follow quickly and in it we will endeavor to do our *duty* to our readers, to ourself and to the villains whom we are warring with

We hope that the morally disposed and those whose *duty* it is to enforce the laws which have been passed to ensure morality, will give us at least, the aid of their good wishes We thank our many patrons for our unexpected, but, we hope not undeserved success

www.ingramcontent.com/pod-product-compliance
Lightning Source LLC
LaVergne TN
LVHW081346060426
835508LV00017B/1442